Be Still, Say Less

Dr. Thurman E. Webb, Jr.

Be Still, Say Less. Copyright 2025 by Dr. Thurman E. Webb, Jr. All rights reserved. No part of this publication may be reproduced, distributed, or transmitted in any form or by any means, including photocopying, recording, or other electronic or mechanical methods, without the prior written permission of the publisher, except in the case of brief quotations embodied in critical reviews and certain other noncommercial uses permitted by copyright law.

For permission requests, write to the publisher, addressed "Attention: Permissions Coordinator," 205 N. Michigan Avenue, Suite #810, Chicago, IL 60601. 13th & Joan books may be purchased for educational, business or sales promotional use. For information, please email the Sales Department at sales@13thandjoan.com.

Printed in the U. S. A.

First Printing, July 2025.

Library of Congress Cataloging-in-Publication Data has been applied for.

ISBN: 978-1-961863-87-3

This book is dedicated to MiAngel (444).

We could debate all day whether the glass is half empty or half full, but what we can agree on is that there's always room for more. Stay focused.

— Dr. Thurman E. Webb, Jr.

Foreword

THIS BOOK IS A GUIDE TO INCREASING YOUR AWARENESS by fostering an honest relationship with yourself. Through that transparency, you can redefine how you build and maintain relationships with others. At its core, this work isn't about offering you yet another "how-to" manual for self-improvement. It's about providing a space for clarity that begins with understanding who you are and holding yourself accountable for what you uncover.

Some might ask, "Do we really need another book like this? Aren't there plenty already out there?" That's a fair question. But what makes this book different is that it's rooted in the experience of navigating the world from a marginalized perspective—a space where clarity isn't always a given and where understanding yourself and your relationships can often be a radical act of survival.

This book is also about communication but not as a tool for persuasion or influence. True communication is about clarity–the courage to understand yourself fully and express that understanding in your connections with others. It's about being honest, even when that honesty is uncomfortable. That's why you'll find reflective honesty questions at the end of each chapter. These questions aren't there to provide easy answers. They're meant to help you confront the truths you might be avoiding and to foster alignment between your thoughts and feelings.

As a counselor and educator, I've seen how often people come to therapy thinking it's about solving problems. In reality, the work is about managing what already exists, coming to grips with the truths we've been avoiding and accepting the responsibility that comes with knowing. Many people resist that responsibility because once you know something, you're accountable for it. But freedom begins with that acknowledgment.

These honesty questions are designed to help you hold yourself accountable in real and meaningful ways. Let's be honest: Sometimes we blame external factors for our repeated patterns. We say, "There are no good partners out there," or "This person just wasn't a good match for me," without looking at why we keep making the same choices. The hard truth is that if you're consistently picking the wrong person or ending up in unhealthy dynamics, there's something within you that needs examination. What are you drawn to, and why does that pattern keep repeating itself?

Inspired by the teachings of Frantz Fanon, this book encourages you to ask essential questions:

- Who am I?
- Am I who I say I am?
- Am I who I ought to be?

When we answer these questions honestly, we often find the information we need to realign ourselves. Alignment is powerful.

It's the moment when the wisdom in your mind aligns with the wisdom in your body. Thoughts are the vocabulary of the mind, and emotions are the vocabulary of the body. When those are in harmony, decision-making becomes clearer, relationships more meaningful, and life less chaotic.

Being out of alignment has consequences: Indecision, inefficiency, living in survival mode rather than thriving in performance mode, and finding ourselves in unproductive relationships. The stomach churns, the mind fogs, and we mislabel our problems without ever addressing their true source.

This book invites you to embark on a journey toward alignment and clarity. It won't provide all the answers, but it will help you ask the right questions. And sometimes, that's all you need to get back on track.

Contents

INTRODUCTION:
Without Commitment, Love Suffocates 1

Part I 5

PILLAR #1:
Shifting from Perception to Perspective 10

PILLAR #2:
The Priceless Currency of Time 15

PILLAR #3:
The Interconnection of Time, Intention, and Impact 21

PILLAR #4:
How Perspective Fuels Motivation 25

PILLAR #5:
Trauma Requires Healing, Not Erasure............................ 29

PILLAR #6:
The Power of Truth, Accountability, and Critical Thinking 35

PILLAR #7:
Courage and Self-Awareness: Building Inner-Resilience 41

PILLAR #8:
The Paradox of Humble Beginnings 47

PILLAR #9:
The Art of Maintenance: Nurturing Awareness and
Responsibility 52

PILLAR #10:
Self-Trust Through Realistic Understanding of Your Limits 57

Part II 69

PILLAR #1:
Curating Connections: Harnessing the Power of Relationships .. 72

PILLAR #2:
The Power of Kindness: Fueling Personal Growth and
Expanding Awareness 77

PILLAR #3:
Turning Dreams into Reality: The Journey of Creation 84

PILLAR #4:
Breaking Boundaries: Expanding Awareness Beyond Limiting
Beliefs 90

PILLAR #5:
The Essence of Love: A Journey of Intentionality and
Purpose 99

PILLAR #6:
From Complacency to Leadership: Stepping into Your
Potential 104

PILLAR #7:
Cultivating Peace and Happiness: A Path to Inner
Harmony 110

PILLAR #8:
Trusting Your Instincts: Ancestral Wisdom for Modern Decisions 117

PILLAR #9:
Confronting the Past: Resolving Unfinished Business 122

PILLAR #10:
Escaping the Trap of Familiarity 128

Debriefing 133

Part III 139

PILLAR #1:
Redefining Success: Embracing Inner Growth 142

PILLAR #2:
Returning to the Authentic Self: A Journey Within 149

PILLAR #3:
Navigating the Spaces that Shape Us 153

PILLAR #4:
Awakening Inner-Strength through Gratitude and Appreciation 157

PILLAR #5:
Unlocking Potential Through Trust and Guidance 161

PILLAR #6:
Harnessing the Power of Connection 166

PILLAR #7:
Branding and Networking: Catalysts for Progress 171

PILLAR #8:
Fueling Personal Growth through Creative Transformation 175

PILLAR #9:
The Strength of Accountability: Owning Your Space 179

PILLAR #10:
Shaping Your Future Through Continuous Learning 182

Part IV 195

PILLAR #1:
The Resilience Path: Cultivating Authentic Growth 198

PILLAR #2:
Collaborative Growth: Unlocking Collective Progress 204

PILLAR #3:
Clarity Through Communication 208

PILLAR #4:
The Power of Empowerment 213

PILLAR #5:
Setting and Maintaining Healthy Boundaries 220

PILLAR #6:
The Essential Strength of Empathy 225

PILLAR #7:
The Vital Practice of Self-Care 229

PILLAR #8:
The Role of Self-Reflection in Growth 234

PILLAR #9:
The Art and Practice of Decision-Making 239

PILLAR #10:
Goal Setting... 244

Part V 257

PILLAR #1:
Cultivating Self-Leadership in a Changing World 260

PILLAR #2:
The Art of Letting Go: Embracing Self-Awareness,
Delegation, and Empowered Leadership 264

PILLAR #3:
Transforming Conflict: Leading Through Creative
Abrasion 268

PILLAR #4:
Harnessing Emotional Intelligence for Personal Growth
and Fulfillment 273

PILLAR #5:
Growing Through Change: The Power of Adaptability 278

PILLAR #6:
Unlocking Potential with a Growth Mindset 284

PILLAR #7:
The Role of Risk-Taking in Personal and Professional
Growth 290

PILLAR #8:
Time Management: Creating Harmony and Achievement 295

PILLAR #9:
The Transformative Power of Public Speaking 300

PILLAR #10:
Gratitude–The Heart of a Fulfilling Life 305

Introduction

Without Commitment, Love Suffocates

PEOPLE OFTEN SAY LOVE IS NOT ENOUGH, HOWEVER, I disagree with this statement. If you grew up in the church like I did, then you believe God is love. And if you believe this is true, then God IS enough. However, while love is beautiful, powerful, and essential, I've come to believe that love, passion, or inspiration—whatever drives you—is not enough without commitment. Commitment is the invisible thread that turns fleeting desires into enduring realities. It's the fuel that powers action long after motivation has left the room.

Commitment isn't flashy, nor is it glamorous. It doesn't thrive on good days or when things are going perfectly. Instead, it quietly holds its ground in the face of doubt, exhaustion, and setbacks. Commitment is the thing that whispers, "Keep going," even when everything in you wants to quit. I didn't fully understand this truth until life demanded that I commit to something bigger than temporary satisfaction—a goal, a calling, a purpose that wouldn't let me off the hook.

If I think back to the first time I ever made a serious

commitment, it was to something surprisingly superficial—a tattoo. I deliberated for weeks, maybe months, about the design and location. Once I sat in that chair and felt the sting of the needle, there was no turning back. That tattoo and I were bound for life, like it or not. That experience planted a seed in my mind about the nature of commitment. It wasn't just a decision. It was a point of no return. You don't get to opt out halfway through when it hurts or when you doubt whether it was a good idea in the first place.

What I didn't realize then was that commitment was not just about enduring something, it was about transforming through it. That understanding didn't fully blossom until later in life when I pursued an advanced degree. In the beginning, I was fueled by excitement and sheer naivete. But that enthusiasm didn't last. Reality hit hard. The late nights, financial stress, and endless revisions to papers threatened to crush my spirit. I wanted to quit more times than I care to admit. But something deeper kept me going—a stubborn resolve that had nothing to do with how I felt in the moment.

Commitment became my guiding light. It allowed me to embrace discomfort as part of the process rather than a reason to abandon the journey. I drew strength from my ancestors, whose resilience was woven into my DNA. They knew hardship intimately, yet they pressed forward. Their endurance became my inspiration, reminding me that some goals are worth the struggle, even when the outcome isn't immediately clear. I learned that sometimes it takes selfishness to become selfless—pushing through personal discomfort for a purpose greater than yourself.

This realization didn't just apply to my academic pursuits. It shaped how I approached everything else in life. I began to see that commitment was the common thread in every success story, whether it was building a business, maintaining health, or cultivating meaningful relationships. But here's the thing: Commitment isn't about perfection. It's about showing up, again and again, despite the imperfections, doubts, and failures. Commitment is a coach yelling in your ear, "Even when it doesn't feel good, get up and put in the work!" It's about making a decision and sticking to it when every cell in your body screams for the easy way out.

Unfortunately, we live in a world that often glorifies instant gratification and overnight success. Social media is filled with highlight reels that make it seem as if everyone is winning effortlessly. What you don't see is the sweat, tears, and relentless commitment behind those wins. What you don't hear are the stories of people who failed, got back up, and kept going until they reached their goals.

Commitment requires discipline, yes, but it also requires faith that your efforts will pay off even when you can't see the results yet. It demands that you trade temporary pleasures for long-term gains. That chocolate cake might taste amazing in the moment, but those rock-hard abs you're working for will taste even sweeter in the end. Sometimes, it's about redefining what success looks like altogether, finding joy in the process rather than just the outcome.

But commitment isn't just a personal endeavor. It's a cultural force that has the power to reshape communities and societies. Imagine a world where people didn't give up so easily on their dreams, their relationships, or their responsibilities. Imagine a world where accountability was celebrated, where sacrifice was seen as worthwhile, and where perseverance was admired more than instant success. Commitment, when practiced collectively, becomes a game-changer. It creates a culture where people lift each other up, where the focus shifts from self-centered pursuits to acts of service and resilience.

This book is an exploration of that transformative power of commitment. Through personal stories, lessons learned, and broader cultural reflections, I invite you to journey with me as we unravel the ways commitment can reshape our lives and the world around us. Because at the end of the day, dreams don't come true just because we want them to. They come true because we commit to making them a reality. That commitment is the bridge between who we are now and who we have the potential to become.

Let's cross that bridge together.

Part I
Beyond the Surface: Exploring

Time, Perspective, and Personal Resilience

REFUSE TO LOSE. THAT COULD HAVE BEEN THE MOTTO that guided my life. The journey to where I stand today wasn't a smooth or easy one. It was endured through hard work, perseverance, and the unwavering belief that I could create something of my own. I can still hear my mother's words ringing in my ears: "One day, you're gonna have your own." Her voice became a source of energy that pushed me forward when times got tough. My story is one of self-discovery, empowerment, and transformation. In the pages that follow, I invite you to come along for the ride. What I've learned, seen, and experienced have shaped the way I live. I hope the lessons I learned can serve as a blueprint for your own path toward greater self-awareness and personal growth.

Life has been a rollercoaster for me, just as it is for many. I've had my share of highs and lows, triumphs and failures. I still remember sitting on a plane as a young boy, staring out the window at the vastness of the Atlantic Ocean, only to return home to a rented room that I shared with my mother. That contrast—a world so big and a space so small—taught me early on that our circumstances don't define us, but they certainly challenge us. I've faced those challenges, and I've overcome them, but it was never easy. Along the way, I've come to realize that navigating life means not just moving through it but rather understanding ourselves, recognizing the power of timing, and being aware of the interplay between our intentions and the time we have.

Self-awareness is at the heart of personal growth and involves far more than just knowing we exist. Far more essential is finding the courage to look deeper into who we are. I've always believed this: "Courageous is the soul who endures the pain of self-discovery." The pain is real, but so is the strength that comes from it. Ultimately, the hope is that we emerge more resilient, more grounded, and more connected to who we truly are.

As we dive into these ideas together, we'll also explore the concept of timing. Timing isn't just something that happens to us but is rather a force we can harness. It can propel us toward success or leave us wondering what could have been. Alongside timing, there's intention. How we spend our time reflects our true intentions. The clearer we are about those intentions, the more aligned we become with our goals and dreams.

Perspective plays a pivotal role in all of this. There's a famous illusion called "My Wife and My Mother-in-Law." While looking at the same picture, some people see a young woman, while others see an old woman. It's all about perspective. The way we choose to see the world shapes how we experience it. A positive perspective can fuel personal growth and resilience, while a negative one can trap us in cycles of pain and defeat. If we've lived through the difficulties–and many of us have–we need to confront the truth that trauma, once it touches us, cannot be erased. But it can be addressed and with the courage to face it head-on, healing becomes possible.

Accountability is another essential part of the journey. In simple terms, we are responsible for our own actions. Growth doesn't happen by accident. It requires ownership, humility, and the understanding that our beginnings don't determine our endings. What I've learned is that transformation often happens in stages. We start out as servants working for others, learning, and growing. As we evolve, we become stewards responsible for not just ourselves but for the world around us. Eventually, we become owners of our lives, our choices, and our destinies. It's a process, a working person's evolution, and it can take you from the ground floor all the way to building something of your own.

This book is meant to be a guide, a companion on your journey toward authenticity, resilience, and personal fulfillment. As we explore the 10 pillars that support authentic living, my hope is that you'll find the insights, the inspiration, and the courage to embrace your own transformation and become all that you were meant to be.

So, here's to your journey. Happy reading, and may the road ahead lead you to a deeper understanding of yourself and the world around you!

1

Shifting from Perception to Perspective

*Courageous is the soul who endures the pain
of self-discovery.*
Dr. Thurman E. Webb, Jr.

INTRODUCTION CONCEPT

After receiving my doctorate, I found myself deeply humbled and standing at a crossroads. The weight of that moment hit me in waves, but not in the way I had imagined. As I walked across the stage, one foot in front of the other, the feeling was more like walking a tightrope. The degree I had worked so hard for, the one I believed would be my crowning achievement, felt like both a triumph and a burden. I was on a high from the accomplishment, yet gasping for air as it dawned on me that I was about to navigate a new path for which I had no vision.

Up until that point, I had thought that earning the degree

meant I had conquered the impossible. I became Dr. Thurman E. Webb, Jr., and in many ways, that felt like a monumental achievement. But as I stood on that stage, my past life flashed before me. The path that led me there was paved by someone else's vision, my mother's. From the moment she divorced my father, she set out to create a new reality for herself and for me. She wasn't content with the cards she had been dealt, and she knew that if we were going to make it, we needed a new vision, a bigger one.

My mother's vision carried me through high school and into college. She was relentless in her pursuit of opportunities for me. She researched grants and strategized how I was going to get into the college arena. We created a plan together. Tennessee State University became our goal. When I graduated with my bachelor's degree, it was proof that we had run that race together. But standing on that stage preparing to receive my doctorate, it became clear to me that while I had crossed one finish line, another race was just beginning. This time, my mother wouldn't be there to guide me.

When my mother passed away two months after receiving my doctorate, she left me with more than just memories. She passed the baton. The poetic nature of that realization didn't make it any easier. I had always run the race according to her plan, her vision. And now, as I looked forward, I realized that I had no plan beyond the degree. I hadn't thought about life after this moment, and that left me feeling more connected than ever to the friends I grew up with, those who couldn't see past 18 years of age or life beyond the boundaries of our neighborhood.

The question, "What's next?" echoed in my mind, dragging me into a place of unfamiliarity. It was a space I hadn't anticipated. I had spent so much time working toward a goal that someone else had set for me, I hadn't stopped to consider what I truly wanted, who I was, or where I was going next.

During my undergraduate years, I hadn't even known who I was or what it would take for me to discover myself. That all started to change when I met Dr. Peter Millet. He helped me create an understanding of my identity and what truly piqued my interest. He helped me craft a plan to get the most out of my undergrad and graduate college experience. He exposed me to resources that would help keep pushing me forward to reach my graduation goal. Looking back, I realize that I didn't earn my doctorate because I had always dreamed of it. I became a doctor because of my mother's vision and the village of support surrounding me. After her cancer diagnosis, it became a shared goal and something that brought her immense joy.

I'll never forget the day I told her I was considering pursuing my doctorate. She was staring out the window and without turning to face me, she simply said, "Man, my only son, a doctor." Those words pierced my soul. My mother was a visionary, a progressive thinker. After having had two miscarriages before me, my birth became her proof that anything was possible. She consequently never saw limitations, only opportunities. She was always pushing me beyond the boundaries of our immediate surroundings, ensuring I saw a world much grander than the one we lived in.

The doctorate became a wall that she wanted me to break through. In her eyes, it wasn't even a wall but just a pile of bricks gathered at my feet–no match for my perseverance. I became the tangible evidence of her faith and her relentless pursuit of possibilities. From the moment I was born, she had envisioned a life of potential for me. Higher education was just one part of her grander vision, and I wanted to achieve that before she passed.

What I hadn't anticipated was how difficult it would be to envision life beyond the degree. I had the drive to start the journey, but finishing required more of me than I had realized. To go the distance, I first had to reduce the anxiety that came with stepping into the unknown. I had to accept that discomfort and uncertainty were natural parts of the process.

It was during this period of reflection that I tapped into a deeper understanding of my ancestry. My ancestors endured unspeakable hardships as they were classified as less than human merely because of their skin color. Yet they not only survived, they thrived. Their contributions to the world became my inheritance. It was their existence that made the impossible possible, and I began to see that I too had the capacity to exceed not only the expectations of others but also my own.

In this spirit, I committed fully to the process of achieving higher education degrees. My efforts became my comfort and my logic, my motivation. Over the years, I've come to deeply value commitment to a process. It's within that space that new potential is born. It's only when we push beyond the boundaries of our own minds that we can tap into the genius that lies just out of reach.

This same principle applies to self-preservation. Many people see self-preservation as merely sustaining oneself, but I believe true preservation happens when we reach for the "more" that's available to us. It's the act of seeing the world and ourselves with a fresh, enlightened vision. To truly become aware of the highest versions of ourselves, we must continuously seek more.

Walking daily in this awareness has allowed someone like me, someone from humble beginnings with limited resources and whose primary identity is one that is marginalized (i.e., Black male), to achieve what many thought was impossible. In the words of Jay-Z, "Difficulty takes a day, impossible takes a week." As I reflect on my journey, I know that the impossible is always within reach. It just requires a vision beyond what we can see today.

2

The Priceless Currency of Time

> *In the modern flux of life, it is not just what we accomplish but when that determines our alignment with opportunity and serendipity.*
> Dr. Thurman E. Webb, Jr.

FATHER TIME IS UNDEFEATED! YET TIME IS THE VARIABLE by which we judge everything. It governs our lives, shaping everything we do–our achievements, growth, and aging. From the moment we are born, time is the backdrop of our existence, and it is relentless in its forward march. Yet over the years, I've come to understand that there are two powerful forces that seem to transcend time's grip: Unwavering commitment and the ever-present concept of "now." These two principles allow us to engage with life in a deeper, more intentional way. They offer a path to living with greater clarity and purpose where time no longer feels like an enemy but a partner in our journey.

There is an old African proverb that says, "No matter how long the night, the day is sure to come." This simple yet profound truth speaks to the inevitability of time's passage, but also to the hope that comes with it. Even in our darkest moments, time marches forward, bringing with it the potential for renewal, growth, and change. What happens in those hours between the night and the dawn depends on how we use them. Will we allow time to pass us by, or will we engage with it meaningfully, using every moment to create the life we desire?

In the early years of my career, I struggled with time. It felt as though it was always slipping through my fingers no matter how hard I tried to keep up. I measured my success by the number of tasks I could complete each day, convinced that maximizing the hours equaled more progress. I was so focused on squeezing productivity out of every minute that I failed to see the bigger picture. I was consequently busy, but I wasn't fulfilled. I was checking off tasks, but I wasn't living with intention. Something had to change.

It was during one of these particularly exhausting periods that I came across a Somali proverb that states, "Wisdom does not come overnight." The truth of this proverb resonated deeply with me. I realized that my approach to time had been rooted in impatience and the illusion that success would come from pushing harder, doing more, and racing against the clock. But wisdom, the kind of wisdom that leads to a fulfilling life, does not come from rushing. It comes from slowing down, from living with intention, and from understanding that the best things in life take time to cultivate.

THE POWER OF COMMITMENT

The first shift in my relationship with time came when I began to understand the power of commitment. Commitment is a force that can render time irrelevant. When you truly commit to something, whether it's a person, a purpose, or a project, you stop obsessing over how long it will take or how much time you have. Instead, your focus shifts to the effort and intention you're putting in. It's in this state of deep commitment that time seems to lose its grip. You're no longer racing to the finish line but rather are immersed in the journey and fully present in the process.

I vividly remember a project that taught me this lesson. I had committed to writing a book, and the deadline loomed over me like a shadow. Every day I sat at my desk, watching the hours slip away, feeling the weight of time pressing down on me. I was constantly aware of the ticking clock, worried about whether I could finish in time. One day, something shifted. I stopped worrying about the deadline and focused solely on the act of writing. I became fully absorbed in the words, in the ideas that flowed onto the page. Time seemed to fade into the background. I wasn't thinking about how much time I had left but instead was simply committed to the process.

That was the moment I understood that commitment isn't just about getting something done. Instead, it is about being fully present in what you're doing. The more deeply I committed to the process, the less time seemed to matter. It became clear that true commitment transcends time because it roots you in the present moment where all that matters is the effort you're exerting.

EMBRACING THE "NOW"

In addition to commitment, I began to recognize the power of the present moment, the "now." We often hear phrases such as "Live in the moment" or "Be present." In our fast-paced world, it's easy to miss the deeper truth behind these words. The present moment is the only place where life truly happens, yet so many of us spend our time dwelling on the past or worrying about the future, missing the richness of the now.

For me, this realization didn't come easily. As a young professional, I was always planning ahead, thinking about the next step, the next achievement, or the next milestone. I believed that success came from being prepared, from staying one step ahead. In doing so, I often missed the beauty and power of what was happening right in front of me. I was always chasing the future, never fully living in the present.

It wasn't until I began practicing mindfulness that I started to understand the true power of the now. I began incorporating small moments of mindfulness into my daily routine, pausing to take a deep breath, noticing the sights and sounds around me, and practicing gratitude for the moment I was experiencing. Slowly, I began to see that life was unfolding in the present, not in the future I had been so focused on. The more I lived in the now, the more connected I felt to my work, my relationships, and my own personal growth.

Living in the present means acting with intention, not out of habit or anxiety. It means recognizing that the only time we can truly act, grow, or change is right now. Once you embrace this truth, time's hold over you loosens. You stop feeling as though time is running out and instead, you begin to experience time as something that supports your journey.

THE IMPORTANCE OF TIMING

While commitment and presence help us transcend the constraints of time, there's another crucial element to our relationship with time and that is the importance of timing. Knowing when to act is just as important as knowing what to do. There's an old saying my mother used to tell me: "You better know what time it is," and she didn't just mean the time of day. She was talking about understanding the dynamics around you, knowing when to act, when to wait, when to speak, and when to listen.

I learned this lesson in a very personal way during my counseling practice. I had a client who was going through a deep period of grief. I had all the right words to say, all the empathy and support I could offer. But as I began to speak, I realized it wasn't the right time. My client wasn't ready to hear comforting words. What they needed in that moment was space to sit with their emotions, to grieve without the pressure of moving on too quickly. If I had pushed forward with my well-meaning advice, it would have fallen flat. Timing matters. Saying the right thing at the wrong time can do more harm than good.

This lesson extended beyond my work with clients. Timing affects every aspect of life from our relationships, our decisions, and our career paths. There have been moments in my life when I pushed too soon, eager for progress, only to find that I wasn't ready or the circumstances weren't aligned. Over time, I've learned to listen to the rhythm of life, to understand when it's time to move forward and when it's time to wait.

TIME AS OUR MOST VALUABLE RESOURCE

Through all of these experiences, I've come to see time as our most valuable resource. Unlike money or material possessions, time is finite. Once it's gone, it's gone forever. We all have the same 24 hours in a day. How we choose to spend those hours determines the quality of our lives.

For years, I believed that success came from working harder, putting in more hours, and constantly pushing myself to do more. What I eventually realized is that reclaiming time by learning to use it more intentionally is what truly brings freedom. Instead of trying to pack more into each day, I began focusing on creating space for what mattered most–relationships, creativity, and self-reflection. This wasn't just about managing my time better. I changed my entire relationship with time.

This shift in perspective has allowed me to live with greater awareness. I've stopped trying to conquer time and have instead learned to work with it. Time will always move forward but when we commit deeply, live in the present, and understand the importance of timing, we can create a life that feels purposeful and aligned with our values.

There is a quote that says, "The best time to plant a tree was 20 years ago. The second-best time is now." This wisdom captures the essence of what I've come to learn. We can't change the past, and we can't predict the future, but we can choose how we engage with the present. We can choose to live with awareness, making the most of the time we have right now.

By embracing the power of commitment, living fully in the now, and learning to master the art of timing, we can reclaim our time and use it to build the life we truly desire. Time is the metric that determines how long our life journey is, but how we choose to engage with it defines the quality of our journey.

3

The Interconnection of Time, Intention, and Impact

*Time is not refundable. Use it wisely, for each moment
spent is an investment in the life you are creating.*
Dr. Thurman E. Webb, Jr.

IN EXPLORING THE INTRICATE RELATIONSHIP BETWEEN time, intention, and impact, I've come to think of time and intention as close relatives like siblings who are inseparable and intertwined by nature. It's not enough to simply have good intentions. To truly shape our lives, our intentions must be matched with well-timed, impactful actions. The responsibility lies not just in setting our intentions but also in ensuring that they land with the power and effect we desire. Does your intention spark a fire? If it doesn't, the message may need reframing or reconstruction to ignite the desired impact. This is where timing becomes pivotal, as a poorly timed action or message can strip away the power of even the most heartfelt intention.

This awareness has been especially revealing during moments

of loss where scripted condolences or well-meaning words often miss the mark. It's in these moments that I've learned the true value of timing and presence. Sometimes the best thing you can offer is your presence, not your words. Well-intentioned expressions can easily come across as insensitive if delivered at the wrong moment. I've found that especially in grief, being there in silence without trying to fill the space with words can make a far deeper impact. There's a fine line between offering support and "doing too much." Learning when to simply be is just as important as knowing what to say.

Why is time considered our most valuable resource? Because time, quite simply, equals life. Wasting time is wasting life. While money can buy conveniences and comforts, it holds no power over time. Once spent, time cannot be reclaimed or replenished. This is why I have a deep respect for people's time, as well as my own. Each moment spent is a moment gone forever. Understanding this truth has transformed the way I approach life. I don't want to waste my time—or anyone else's.

Do we control the time we're granted, or does time control us? It's a question that often arises when we think about the finite nature of our lives. While we may exert some influence over how we spend our time, none of us knows exactly how much time we have. We all have a predetermined expiration date, though it's not something we're conscious of on a daily basis. This brings the focus away from how much time we have and toward how we spend the time that is given to us. The art of living, then, is rooted in becoming keenly aware of how we navigate time, using it to create meaningful moments and impactful outcomes.

One of the great equalizers in life is that we all receive the same 24 hours each day. The question becomes not how to accumulate more time, but how to maximize the time we have.

Imagine completing a task that typically takes eight hours in just four. Now imagine completing it in two. The goal is not simply to work faster but to reclaim time, creating more options and opportunities in the process. When I realized this, my entire perspective shifted. Time, not money, became the true currency of my life. Money, as I now see it, is a tool, a means to create convenience and to buy back time. This revelation struck me as I observed successful individuals who placed as much value on their time as they did on their wealth. For instance, chartering a private jet wasn't about extravagance but about saving time. They understood that the hours spent waiting at an airport was time that could be spent creating more opportunities or deepening their success.

Entrepreneur Jim Rohn once said, "Time is more valuable than money. You can get more money, but you cannot get more time." His words echo the reality that time is finite. We consequently must make intentional choices about how we spend it. The implications of not being intentional are profound. Without intentionality, it's easy to waste hours getting lost in distractions—whether scrolling through social media or falling into the black hole of entertainment. You can watch countless videos of Bigfoot sightings, or you can create something that adds value to others' lives. This is the difference between consuming time and using it to create a positive impact.

Many people believe that success is a result of luck or coincidence, but this mindset often masks a lack of intentional action. It's an excuse to avoid the discomfort of potential failure. The reality is when we don't set clear intentions, we often find ourselves reacting rather than responding to life's challenges. This is where intentionality meets ownership. Reflecting on your decisions, owning the information you had at the time, and learning from the experience helps foster growth. It's not about owning the entire situation but rather, owning your role and your influence within it.

There's a crucial difference between responding and reacting. Responses are rooted in proactive energy, requiring thoughtful consideration, while reactions are often driven by heightened emotions. Mastering the ability to respond, and to do so swiftly, can be the difference between making a wise decision and one you might later regret. Those who handle high-stakes situations with grace and precision have learned this skill as they respond so quickly that it mimics the speed of a reaction but with the wisdom of reflection.

This brings us back to the power of intentionality. Being intentional in our actions allows us to align our thoughts with our behaviors, creating clarity and direction. Intentional living means we are deliberate with how we spend our time, how we invest our energy, and how we respond to life's challenges. It's a process of reclaiming time, using it wisely, and unlocking the potential that lies within each moment.

In the end, time, intention, and impact are intricately woven together. Without intentionality, time slips away unnoticed and our actions lose their potency. With clear intention, every moment becomes an opportunity to shape our lives, create meaningful impact, and move closer to our highest potential. The journey of self-awareness and personal growth is, in essence, a journey of reclaiming time, aligning our intentions with our actions, and realizing the profound influence we have over our own lives.

4

How Perspective Fuels Motivation

*I don't develop a Plan A and a Plan B, there is only Plan A.
If I need a plan B, to me that means I didn't put enough
into Plan A.*
Dr. Thurman E. Webb, Jr.

GROWING UP, I HAD ANGER ISSUES. I WAS OFTEN QUIET ON the outside to maintain peace but inside, there was a war raging. I didn't realize it at the time, but bottling up emotions only intensified them. My unresolved triggers would surface unexpectedly, often in explosive reactions that led me to treat people as if they were the cause of my problems. It took years for me to understand that my anger wasn't just about the situations I faced. It was about how I responded to them.

I eventually learned that vulnerability wasn't a weakness but a strength that allowed me to process my emotions rather than react impulsively. Junior year of high school marked a pivotal moment for me. There was an incident where I was bullied. I remember the anger rising within me, the same old patterns of reaction waiting to unfold. But something shifted in me that day. I realized that I couldn't control how others perceived me or what they said, but I could control my response. I decided to act with self-control instead of letting my emotions dictate my actions. That was the moment I began to understand the power of self-awareness.

"Control your emotions, or they will control you." This line from an urban philosopher struck me deeply and over time, I internalized it. Self-awareness and self-control became essential tools in navigating my life, giving me a sense of empowerment I never knew I had. It wasn't about suppressing my feelings but rather acknowledging them and making conscious choices about how to respond.

One concept that has shaped my understanding of time and emotions is the distinction between urgency and importance. Urgency is often driven by external pressures—other people's demands, stress, or the sense of feeling overwhelmed because of too much to do. Importance, on the other hand, is aligned with your own goals and values. I learned that most of the time, people confuse the two. They let the urgency of the moment dictate their actions but in doing so, they sacrifice what's truly important. Understanding this distinction allowed me to pause, reflect, and decide whether I needed to react to a situation or respond with intention.

As I started to practice this awareness, I noticed a common human tendency: We create stories to fill in the gaps when we don't have all the facts. Imagination, which can be a gift, often becomes a breeding ground for misinformation, assumptions, and drama. We create narratives based on incomplete information, leading to misunderstandings and misjudgments. This is known as the fundamental attribution error—our tendency to make quick judgments about others' behavior without considering the full picture.

How often have we been guilty of reacting to someone based on a story we created in our heads? The danger lies in the fact that these stories are influenced by our own insecurities, biases, and emotional triggers. Taking time to reflect on what we don't know and seeking clarity rather than jumping to conclusions fosters a more realistic and compassionate understanding of ourselves and others.

Interviewing people about their struggles, weaknesses, and moments of quitting has revealed just how essential self-awareness is for growth. When people are honest about their limitations and confront their failures, they become more equipped to solve problems realistically. Facing the uncomfortable aspects of ourselves—the parts we'd rather ignore—provides the clearest path to self-awareness. When we don't know something, it's tempting to fill in the blanks with assumptions. Spending time reflecting on what we don't know and questioning our initial reactions leads to informed decisions and a more grounded understanding of reality.

This principle extends far beyond personal relationships. For example, exploring the brutal history of enslaved people requires confronting uncomfortable, painful truths. Rather than face the full reality of this history, many people choose to stop at what feels manageable. They downplay the horrors of slavery, gaslighting the situation by saying that enslaved people "learned skills" that helped them. This conveniently ignores the horrific violence and dehumanization that defined that period. They avoid discussing the lynchings that were so rampant in the South that an Anti-Lynching Bill was proposed—and voted down—by Congress, allowing the practice to continue without harsher penalties. They don't talk about the systemic rape or the unspeakable damage caused by ripping Black families apart as mothers, fathers, and children were sold to separate plantations.

This selective understanding of history does a disservice not only to the truth but to our collective growth as a society. Confronting uncomfortable truths, however painful, is essential for breaking down misconceptions and enriching our understanding of the world.

"People will do anything to avoid the hard work of knowing themselves," said another urban philosopher. It's true. Self-awareness, whether on a personal level or a societal level, requires us to face hard realities. It's easier to turn away, to ignore the things that challenge our assumptions. Without this awareness, however, we cannot grow.

Self-awareness demands that we acknowledge the limitations of our imagination. It requires us to confront uncomfortable truths and question the stories we tell ourselves. Only then can we make informed decisions, understand ourselves more deeply, and grow into the people we are meant to be. The journey to self-awareness is a long one, but is the key to unlocking our full potential.

5

Trauma Requires Healing, Not Erasure

> *Embracing your trauma is not about glorifying the pain but recognizing its role in shaping who you are.*
> Dr. Thurman E. Webb, Jr.

GROWING UP IN THE STRUGGLE, I LEARNED EARLY ON THAT our experiences have an undeniable influence on the choices we make, the way we see the world, and the way we interact with others. Poverty leads to aggression. Eat or be eaten. No time to be soft or passive. Trust no one. It's every man for himself in the streets. And you've ALWAYS got to look over your shoulder because someone will try to take what you have. The weight of those experiences, especially trauma, is not something you can disassociate from. Trauma doesn't just fade into the background or disappear over time. It's a force that imprints itself on our thoughts, emotions, and behaviors. For many people, the instinct is to distance themselves from their trauma, suppress it, or deny its impact. I learned through my own journey and from observing others that real growth and change only happen when you confront trauma head-on and accept how it has shaped your life.

In my community, particularly among the Black men and women I saw in the eastern neighborhoods of my city, trauma was an invisible force driving so many decisions. It affected everything from relationships to work ethic, from self-worth to the ability to plan for the future. For some people, trauma led to a mindset of survival and resulted in an inability to think past immediate circumstances. Planning for the future felt pointless when past experiences had shown them that nothing really changed. For others, unresolved trauma manifested as a sense of hopelessness, a belief that nothing they did truly mattered. I saw how this unresolved pain held people back and was passed from one generation to the next, creating a cycle where trauma begets more trauma.

The turning point for me came when I realized that healing and change start with one simple but profound step, namely acceptance. Acceptance is the foundation of personal growth and without it, we remain trapped in the patterns created by our past. But acceptance isn't easy. It requires looking at situations, people, and ourselves without illusion, without idealizing or distorting reality to fit a narrative we find more comfortable. It means acknowledging things as they are—flaws, limitations, and all.

In my journey, I found that acceptance isn't about giving up or resigning ourselves to pain or hardship. Rather, it's about facing the truth so that we can begin to work with it and ultimately transcend it. When I started to observe the natural world, I realized that nature has profound lessons in acceptance. Animals, for example, coexist by accepting each other's presence. They understand their roles, their limits, and their strengths. A lion doesn't waste time wishing it were a bird, and a gazelle doesn't pretend it can outfight a predator. Instead, each creature works within its reality, adapting and surviving. Humans, on the other hand, often struggle to accept one another as we truly are. We interact not with the reality of individuals, but with the ideas we create about them.

One of the most significant lessons I learned came from my personal relationships. I remember a woman I was deeply attracted to. She was beautiful and in my eyes, that beauty overshadowed everything else. I overlooked qualities in her that, if I had been honest with myself, I would have seen weren't aligned with what I truly needed or wanted. I idealized her, choosing to ignore the negative aspects of her personality such as her lack of empathy and constant negativity because I didn't want to confront the truth.

Eventually, I couldn't ignore the truth any longer. Accepting her for who she really was and not who I wanted her to be was a painful but necessary step. In that moment, I understood that real acceptance often involves **distinguishing between facts and emotions.** My emotions were real, as I felt love, attraction, and desire. But they didn't change the reality of her character. I realized that in order to make decisions that served my well-being, I had to accept the truth of the situation, not the story my emotions wanted to tell.

This process of acceptance—whether in relationships, when confronting trauma, or going through daily life—requires us to manage our emotions effectively. Emotions are powerful and undeniably real, but they can sometimes cloud our judgment. The stories we tell ourselves, shaped by these emotions, may not always align with the objective truth. We need to learn how to separate our emotional reactions from the facts to avoid letting our feelings lead us into distorted perceptions.

When I started to truly understand this concept, it changed the way I made decisions. I began to check myself regularly by asking, "Am I reacting based on how I feel, or am I responding to what's really happening?" This shift in thinking brought me a new level of clarity and awareness. It helped me make better choices, whether it was in personal relationships or in professional endeavors. It's not that emotions are wrong or something to be dismissed. They are important and provide valuable insights, but they shouldn't be the sole drivers of our actions.

Acceptance also plays a crucial role in how we process information and navigate complex situations. One of the hardest truths to accept is that **we are not the absolute truth.** Our perspective, while valid, is just one layer of the truth. There are always deeper layers, and other people's perspectives bring valuable dimensions to any situation. This is something that became clear to me when I started engaging in conversations with people who had vastly different life experiences than mine.

At first, it was difficult. I wanted to defend my point of view and assert that what I believed was the only truth. But the more I listened, the more I realized that **truth is multifaceted.** My experiences shaped my understanding, but other people's experiences shaped theirs. Both could be true in different ways. This understanding opened my eyes to the importance of welcoming new information and being willing to evolve my perspective as I encountered new truths.

I saw this struggle often in the people around me, especially those grappling with trauma. Trauma can make us rigid, clinging to our version of reality as a form of protection. It feels safer to hold on to what we know, even if it's painful, than open ourselves up to the discomfort of new perspectives. Real change, real growth, only happens when we are willing to step into that discomfort. When we acknowledge that our truth is one piece of a larger puzzle, we create space for healing and for deeper understanding.

Navigating the journey of change is no small feat, especially when trauma and poverty are part of the equation. The communities I came from were filled with individuals carrying heavy burdens shaped by systemic inequalities and personal hardships. How do you ask for help when you don't trust the system? Health disparities in our neighborhood are easily proven by the lack of resources available in our community and the higher rates of heart disease, stroke, cancer and asthma. Imagine the same group of Black people who were injected with syphilis and essentially experimented on by the US government until 1974 during the Tuskegee Experiment lining up to get vaccinated against Covid-19 in 2021. Of course, the mental damage is still there. Unresolved trauma compounded by financial struggle creates an environment where it feels nearly impossible to move forward. Even in the face of these challenges, I learned that change is possible, and it starts with acceptance.

Acceptance doesn't mean we condone injustice or resign ourselves to suffering. Instead, it means we stop denying or distorting reality and begin to work with what is in front of us. We can't create meaningful change from a place of illusion. When we accept the truth of our circumstances, no matter how difficult, we become empowered to find realistic solutions. We stop wasting energy on wishing things were different and instead use that energy to create change where it's possible.

Another powerful lesson I learned was that **acceptance doesn't mean we stop striving for more.** In fact, it's the opposite. Acceptance is the foundation that allows us to grow, to push for progress, and to step into personal transformation. Once we accept where we are, we can begin to chart a path toward where we want to go. This process involves managing our emotions, staying open to evolving truths, and being honest about the role trauma plays in shaping our decisions.

In reflecting on my own journey, I can see how each step of growth was rooted in some form of acceptance. Whether it was accepting the truth of a relationship, the limitations imposed by trauma, or the reality of my community's struggles, each moment of clarity moved me closer to personal freedom. Acceptance, in its truest form, is an act of courage. It requires us to face ourselves and our circumstances without flinching, to see things as they are rather than as we wish them to be.

In the journey of personal growth, acceptance is not the end but rather the beginning. It's the moment when we stop fighting against reality and start working with it. It's the point where we recognize that our experiences, while powerful, do not define our future unless we let them. It's the guiding light that helps us navigate the shadows of trauma, poverty, and all the other challenges life throws our way.

As we step into this journey of growth, let us remember that acceptance isn't about giving up. It's about facing the truth so that we can move forward stronger and more aware than before. When we embrace acceptance of ourselves, our emotions, and the world around us, we unlock the potential for real transformation. And that's where personal growth truly begins.

6

The Power of Truth, Accountability, and Critical Thinking

Accountability and self-awareness are the cornerstones of personal growth. One keeps us honest, while the other keeps us mindful.
Dr. Thurman E. Webb, Jr.

As we navigate through this race called life, three pit stops along the way can help us reach our destination: Truth, accountability, and critical thinking. These elements form the foundation of personal growth, self-awareness, and authentic leadership. If you pay close attention, you'll recognize their immense value, especially when life's choices become difficult or when the consequences of our actions loom large. The ability to weave together our past experiences with our present realities is what ultimately defines who we are.

"Our ability to blend the past and the present defines our

identity" is a truth I often share with my students. To understand who we are and where we're going, we must be honest about yesterday. Healing begins with acknowledging our wounds, not burying them beneath layers of illusion or avoidance. We cannot fill the pages of our history with faded memories and colored lines drawn by our imagination. Accountability sharpens the contours of our past, giving us the clarity needed to move forward.

Accountability often feels heavy. It's not that we are afraid of failure. More often, it's the discomfort of facing the reality that our actions carry consequences that might challenge the image we hold of ourselves. Many shy away from accountability because it demands honesty—sometimes uncomfortable, sometimes humbling, but always necessary. To hold oneself accountable is to stand in front of a mirror, free of distortions, and acknowledge not only where we have succeeded but where we have fallen short.

I once had a conversation with a colleague about this reluctance to confront truth. She shared a powerful insight: "People don't fear failure as much as they fear the consequences of their actions. That acknowledgment forces us to recalibrate how we see ourselves, and that's not easy." This resonated deeply with me as I reflected on my own past, the decisions I made, and the moments I avoided accepting responsibility because it would have required me to reassess who I believed I was. Accountability, however, is the lens through which we gain clarity about our identity and integrity.

TRUTH: THE BEDROCK OF GROWTH

Andre 3000, a legend in the world of hip-hop, once said in a song, "Keep your heart, 3 Stacks. Keep your heart." The lyrics highlight an essential truth about vulnerability, especially in the realm of love and commitment. Vulnerability doesn't mean weakness but rather being open and honest with ourselves about who we are, what we want, and the risks we're willing to take. Love, like accountability, is not just a fleeting emotion but a commitment—a deliberate and purposeful act. Yet many people shy away from choosing love or committing to anything at all, paralyzed by the fear of possible hurt or disappointment.

In my own life, I've wrestled with this fear. There were times when I held back from fully engaging in relationships or from committing to a decision because I feared what might come. The imagined hurt felt too great. I chose the safer path—the lesser pain—believing that avoiding vulnerability would protect me. In reality, all I did was shackle myself to stagnation. In the absence of truth, I was unable to grow. The false comfort of avoidance only deepened my discontent.

Similarly, in our everyday lives, we often protect ourselves from perceived failure by avoiding truth. We hide behind our excuses, rationalizations, or selective memories. A student once asked me, "Why do we try to forget?" The question was poignant. We try to forget because we want to present the best version of ourselves to the world, even if it's not the whole truth. We curate our memories, shading over the parts of ourselves we're ashamed of, convinced that others will only accept us if we seem perfect.

Here's the truth: Perfection is a myth. Pursuing perfection often leads to self-deception. In the process, we become trapped in a cycle of toxic self-absorption fueled by shame, guilt, and societal pressures that tell us we are not enough. This leads to selective memory, where we try to forget our past mistakes or failures rather than face them, learn from them, and use them to grow.

ACCOUNTABILITY: THE KEY TO SELF-DISCOVERY

Real accountability begins when we stop running from the truth. It requires us to embrace the parts of ourselves that we might not like, to face the reality that our choices have consequences, and to take responsibility for those consequences. When we are accountable, we are no longer bound by the past. We become free to shape our future with intention and awareness.

I think of a time in my own life when I avoided taking responsibility for a decision that impacted a close friendship. I justified my actions, telling myself that I had been right, that I was the victim of circumstance. Deep down, I knew that wasn't the case. I had made a poor choice, and my friend had been hurt because of it. It wasn't until I finally held myself accountable that I could begin to repair the damage. I had to admit to myself—and to my friend—that I was wrong. That process, though painful, was freeing. It taught me that accountability isn't about self-punishment but self-awareness.

When we hold ourselves accountable, we accept that our decisions—both good and bad—shape our lives. We stop blaming others for our failures or misfortunes and start looking inward, asking ourselves how we can grow from the experience.

CRITICAL THINKING: NAVIGATING COMPLEXITY WITH CLARITY

Alongside truth and accountability, critical thinking is the third pit stop that guides us through life. Critical thinking requires us to question assumptions, analyze situations from multiple perspectives, and make decisions based on evidence rather than emotion. It's not about finding the "right" answer but exploring all the possibilities before arriving at a well-informed conclusion.

In a world full of distractions, we often rely on easy answers or allow our emotions to dictate our actions. Critical thinking challenges us to slow down, pause, and evaluate information carefully. It's about making decisions with clarity and intent rather than reacting impulsively or emotionally.

I recall a time when I made a hasty decision based on my emotions only to realize later that I had overlooked crucial facts. It was a business decision, one that seemed right in the moment because my excitement clouded my judgment. After a few weeks, I began to see the flaws in my choice. I hadn't thought it through. I hadn't critically examined the situation from all angles. That mistake cost me time, money, and energy, but it also taught me the importance of slowing down and thinking deeply before making decisions.

Critical thinking also reminds us that we are not the ultimate truth. Our perspectives are valid, but they are just one piece of a much larger puzzle. When we engage with others—whether it's in conversations, collaborations, or conflicts—we must remember that other perspectives are equally valid and that understanding those perspectives can enrich our own understanding.

EMBRACING VULNERABILITY AS A PATH TO GROWTH

If truth, accountability, and critical thinking are the building blocks of personal growth, then vulnerability is the mortar that binds them together. It's in vulnerability that we find the courage to face our truths, hold ourselves accountable, and challenge our assumptions. Vulnerability means shedding the masks we wear to protect ourselves and standing in our authenticity.

When I think about vulnerability, I am reminded of something I once heard: "Even if you don't know how to swim, jump into the waters of vulnerability." This is where we discover who we truly are. In the act of being vulnerable, we present ourselves to the world as whole beings—flawed and imperfect but authentic. We stop hiding behind pretenses and start living in alignment with our true selves.

True leaders understand the power of vulnerability. They know that leadership is not about making perfect decisions but about having the courage to make decisions, learn from them, and evolve. Vulnerability allows leaders to be accountable, admit when they're wrong, and inspire others by showing that growth is a continual process.

LIVING THE TRIFECTA

As we move through life, it's easy to avoid the hard work of truth, accountability, and critical thinking. It's easier to stay comfortable, avoid risk, and cling to the stories we've told ourselves. True growth requires that we do the opposite and embrace the trifecta of truth, accountability, and critical thinking—the guiding lights that lead us to greater awareness and deeper personal fulfillment.

In the end, we must shed our insecurities, face our fears, and step into the waters of vulnerability. This is where we discover our authenticity, where we strip away the contradictions, and where we begin to live fully in the present. When we commit to these principles, we create space for personal growth, deeper relationships, and a more meaningful life.

7

Courage and Self-Awareness: Building Inner-Resilience

Fear is the whisper that tells us we're human.
Courage is the roar that reminds us we can rise above it.
Dr. Thurman E. Webb, Jr.

THERE IS A PROFOUND CONNECTION BETWEEN COURAGE and the authentic self. Real courage isn't just the act of standing up in the face of danger or speaking out in a moment of adversity. Its roots run far deeper and are grounded in the exploration of self. Such an expedition demands stillness, solitude, and a willingness to journey inward. It is in those quiet moments away from the noise of the world that free thoughts begin to take shape, personal preferences are discovered, and one's true essence begins to emerge.

I've often reflected on how solitude played a role in shaping my identity, my sense of self, and ultimately my courage. It's a space that many avoid because it forces us to confront parts of ourselves we'd rather not see. For me, it was in those moments of stillness that I began to truly know myself. I began to understand my love language, how I needed to be treated, how I needed to care for myself, and how I could bring my authentic self into the world. Through this self-discovery, I learned that courage isn't just an outward display of bravery but rather an inward journey. You sharpen your essence, refine your spirit, and prepare yourself for the inevitable challenges that life will throw your way.

And yet, amidst all this self-discovery, you must constantly remind yourself: **You are valued.** This value, the core of who you are, must be safeguarded because the world will often try to diminish it. Mainstream society has long struggled to understand the intrinsic value that exists within communities of color, particularly within Black communities. This strength, this resilience, runs through our veins as it has been passed down from our ancestors. It's something our counterparts notice but can never quite comprehend. Our resilience is innate, like melanin. They cannot fathom how a community, despite enduring immense hardship, continues to thrive. The secret isn't in the external but instead within the unyielding resilience of the soul, something they couldn't destroy no matter how hard they tried.

I remember an elder from my community once told me that the relentless pursuit and oppression of people of African descent was rooted in one thing: The inability to decipher the secret of our existence. The colonizers could not break us because our soul was untouched by external forces. Our spirit, though battered by struggle and strife, remained intact, indestructible. Generations of attempts to erase us from history, to silence our voices, failed because our oppressors never understood the depth of our resilience.

There was a somber note in that elder's voice. He spoke of the younger generation and how the internal strength, the courage found within, was under siege—not by external forces, but by our own failure to engage with the self. The internal locus of control, the understanding that we are the masters of our fate and the authors of our stories, was becoming clouded. The layers of self, so essential to our identity, were being buried beneath distractions, societal pressures, and the need for external validation. If we fail to sift through these layers, the elder warned, we risk losing the essence of who we are.

The ancestors, he reminded me, believed that we die three times. The first death is physical, when the body ceases to function. The second is when the last person who knew us dies, and our memory lives only in the minds of others. The third, and most final death, is the last time our name is spoken. This idea weighed heavily on me. What legacy would I leave behind? Would my name survive the generations? Would my essence, my courage, my truth, continue to resonate long after I was gone?

These thoughts forced me to confront my own journey to self-awareness. How did I reach this place of knowing? How did I cultivate the courage to stand in my truth, even when it felt like the world was against me?

I've always been different. Even as a child, I sensed the uniqueness of energies around me. I could read people's dispositions with an almost instinctual accuracy, an intuitive gift that separated me from those around me. My mother was the only other person I knew who shared this awareness and connection to the unseen. While others may have possessed the same gift, it was my acceptance of it that set me apart. I embraced the solitude that came with being different and through that solitude, I found strength.

I still remember those Sunday mornings alone, sitting in my room, while my mom was at the laundromat. I would create entire fantasy worlds, traveling through imaginary stories in my mind. In those moments, I wasn't just entertaining myself but rather building a relationship with myself. Those hours of solitude allowed me to connect with the deeper parts of who I was. The stories I told myself were filled with hope, courage, and resilience. I was learning, even then, how to speak my own love language, how to affirm my worth, and how to understand my place in the world.

That early connection with myself has been the guiding light in my journey. It's what allowed me to step into adulthood with a sense of self that has remained unshaken by the trials of life. The awareness I cultivated as a child and nurtured in moments of solitude blossomed into a powerful force as I grew older. It's this awareness that continues to shape my decisions, relationships, and understanding of the world. Though the journey of self-awareness is a continual process, I am thankful for the foundation that was laid during those quiet childhood Sundays.

I carry this self-awareness with me not as a burden but a beacon. It guides me through the complexities of life, helping me discern what is true from what is false and what is real from what is imagined. It has allowed me to navigate a world that often seeks to silence the voices of those who dare to be different, to be authentic.

This journey and continual discovery of self is not just about me. It's about understanding the connection between my story and the stories of those who came before me. The strength of my ancestors reverberates through my soul. Their courage, their resilience and their wisdom are the gifts they passed down generation after generation. It is our responsibility to honor those gifts by living authentically, embracing the courage to be ourselves, and understanding that our true power lies within.

There is an unspoken truth in Black communities that has

sustained us through centuries of oppression: "Our resilience is not just a product of survival. It is a celebration of life." The statement recognizes that no matter what the world throws our way, we possess an internal strength that cannot be broken. It is this strength that has allowed us to continue to thrive, to create, to love, and to rise above the hardships we've endured.

Yet in today's world, we face a new challenge. The distractions of modern life, the pressures to conform, the constant barrage of messages telling us that we are not enough are all forces that threaten to sever our connection to self, to numb us to the power that lies within. We must resist this. We must reclaim our solitude, our moments of stillness, and use them to reconnect with the essence of who we are.

In my journey, I have learned that true courage comes from within. It is found in the quiet moments of reflection, in the acceptance of one's authentic self, and in the acknowledgment that our value does not depend on external validation. It is the recognition that we are enough, just as we are.

I urge you to not simply walk the path of self-discovery but to **inhabit** it fully. Strip away the veils that obscure who you truly are. Step into the world not as a shadow of yourself but with the unshakable presence of your authentic being. In this act of courage, you do more than claim your own space. You call upon the echoes of those who came before you and those whose breath still lingers in the wind, whose unbreakable spirits have shaped the very ground you stand on.

Toni Morrison once said, "You are your best thing." Let that truth anchor you. To live fully in your own skin is not a defiance of the past but a continuation of it, a way of honoring every ancestor who survived for you to exist. Their resilience is etched into your bones. By owning your story, by carrying the weight of your truth into the world, you become the embodiment of their strength, their wisdom, and their hope. You are not alone in this journey. You are the culmination of generations, a living testament to their courage.

In shedding what no longer serves you—the masks, the imposed narratives, the limitations—you free not only yourself but you also break open the possibility for those around you to do the same. To walk with the full weight of your authenticity is to walk with power, grace, and an unyielding connection to something much greater than yourself. This is how legacies are kept alive. This is how the soul remains unbroken.

8

The Paradox of Humble Beginnings

> *Humble beginnings often carry the highest cost, not in currency, but in resilience, determination, and the unwavering spirit to rise above adversity.*
> Dr. Thurman E. Webb, Jr.

BACK IN THE 80S, THERE WAS A POPULAR "YO' MAMA" JOKE that went, "Your mother is so poor, she can't pay attention." At the time, it was clever wordplay but for me growing up in humble beginnings, it carried a heavier truth. The idea that awareness and attention could come with a price resonated with me in ways I didn't fully understand then but have now come to grasp. I learned early that paying attention, becoming aware, and truly understanding yourself in the world costs you something. Those costs often come in ways you don't anticipate—financially, emotionally, and spiritually.

Reflecting on my journey from those modest beginnings, I now see that every precious moment of self-discovery, every instance of intimacy with myself and others, came at a price.

Awareness was not given freely but rather was earned through struggle, reflection, and the unpacking of life's experiences.

As I grew older, the realization struck me that these moments of clarity and deepened awareness didn't come out of nowhere. They were crafted over time, piece by piece, as I sifted through the baggage I had accumulated through childhood, adolescence, and into adulthood. Watching my mother, I learned a broader truth about life: People need help. Not just her, but everyone. We are all navigating our own journeys, and each of us requires unique forms of support to get through. Life, I began to understand, is like a highway with multiple lanes. We all occupy different lanes at different times, shaped by our individual experiences yet moving in parallel toward the same destination all while trying to make sense of the world and our place in it.

At some point, I declared to myself, "I don't ever want s*** to feel like old times." I didn't want to be weighed down by the same struggles, the same heaviness I had known growing up. The weariness of those early years fueled a fierce determination in me to change, to evolve, and to move beyond what I had known. It wasn't until I was in my 30s that I realized I had actually been homeless on four different occasions. The funny thing is, I didn't recognize it at the time. It wasn't the kind of homelessness people typically think of as there were no nights spent sleeping in a car, no shelters. Instead, we were "staying" with people, sharing a room in their homes. The insulation my mother provided shielded me from fully understanding our reality.

I found myself wondering whether I had chosen to ignore that reality or if my mother had intentionally kept the truth hidden from me. Either way, it became clear that there are different ways of being homeless, just as there are different ways of being aware.

Sometimes, awareness is something you choose and other times, it's something you are protected from.

A trip to Australia became a pivotal milestone in my life—a moment that represented both sacrifice and opportunity. My mother managed to pay for private school at home that seemed beyond her means, and then paid for the trip of a lifetime to Australia, which seemed worlds apart from the experiences of my peers and even from my own experiences of homelessness. That dissonance was part of the lesson. My mother's vision, so much bigger than the immediate challenges we faced, charted a course toward a future that neither of us could fully see. Her love for me drove her to sacrifice things I wasn't even aware she was giving up. For her, moments of deficiency. For me, moments of abundance. It was love that carried us forward and love that crafted a roadmap for me to experience so much more.

I learned through this that life is filled with contradictions. The unity of opposites became a guiding principle for me. Two seemingly contradictory truths can coexist in the same space. It's possible to be in need and to have wealth at the same time. It's possible to feel vulnerable and powerful simultaneously. It's possible to feel lost and be exactly where you need to be.

One day, this principle was challenged in a way I didn't expect. In a classroom, I found myself defending the ideology of a specific fascist–Hitler. It sounds absurd now but at the time, I thought I was defending love. He loved his people, I reasoned, just as I love mine. I was misguided. Rightfully so, my teacher admonished me and made clear what atrocities were committed in the name of that twisted ideology. What I came to realize was that love, if not properly understood, could be manipulated, misused, and turned into something dangerous. I was wrestling with the complex nature of love, discovering that while it is one of the most powerful forces in existence, it can also be used as a weapon.

Through that experience, I learned a critical lesson about love: When accessed through beingness, love is so powerful that it softens all other emotions. It allows you to accept even the hardest emotions—fear, anger, grief—and gather information from them rather than react impulsively. Love, when pure and authentic, informs your decision-making process and guides you toward responses versus reactions. This understanding of love allowed me to see beyond the superficial and embrace the deeper complexities of human emotion and behavior.

It wasn't until much later that I confessed to myself that I didn't realize I hadn't been heartbroken until I had been heartbroken. That realization highlighted something I had known for a long time but hadn't fully articulated: I had lived a life that was both simple and complex. Growing up, people often told me my thought process was peculiar. I saw the world differently, and that difference sometimes felt isolating. I've come to understand that this difference is my strength. The discomfort of trying to fit into a mold of "normalcy" only pushed me further toward embracing who I truly am—someone who has walked through the fire of self-discovery and come out the other side more aware, more grounded, and more connected to my authentic self.

The journey from my humble beginnings was not easy. It was expensive in ways that go far beyond money. It cost me relationships, comfort, and often the sense of belonging. But the price I paid for my awareness and authenticity was well worth it. In shedding the masks that were expected of me, I found the freedom to live a life that is fully my own.

Through this journey, I learned that you have to be willing to pay the cost if you want to live authentically. You have to unpack the baggage, confront the uncomfortable truths, and be willing to navigate the contradictions. It's in doing this hard work that you discover who you are, what you value, and what you're capable of achieving. When you come to that understanding, you realize that the price of awareness is not a burden but an investment in yourself, your future, and the legacy you'll leave behind.

As I reflect now, I see that awareness is both a privilege and a responsibility. It's something you must constantly work toward and share with others. The more aware you become, the more you can guide those around you to their own self-discovery. That's the beauty of this journey. It's never just about you. It's about the people you touch along the way, the lessons you pass on, and the awareness you help cultivate in others. The cost of living authentically, of being fully aware, is high. But it's worth every penny.

9

The Art of Maintenance: Nurturing Awareness and Responsibility

> *Fulfillment isn't found in the destination, but in the daily care of your peace, happiness, and purpose.*
> *It's through this continual stewardship of self that true meaning in life is cultivated.*
> Dr. Thurman E. Webb, Jr.

EVERYTHING IN LIFE REQUIRES MAINTENANCE. YOUR peace and your happiness are not static. They require constant nurturing and care. Understanding this simple yet profound truth is the beginning of a transformative journey of self-discovery. This awareness is where growth begins, where the desire for a meaningful, fulfilled life takes root. I often draw parallels between this realization and the mindset of athletes. There's a difference between merely wanting success and being willing to put in the relentless effort required to achieve it. The distinction lies not in the desire itself but in the commitment to the maintenance necessary to sustain it.

The essence of maintenance is what we do day in and day out to demonstrate our appreciation for what we want. It is where responsibility meets action. To have a desire is one thing but the ongoing and often quiet work that follows is where the real magic happens. Maintenance isn't glamorous, but it is where transformation is born. The act of maintaining something—whether it's your peace, happiness, or success—requires dedication, effort, and most importantly, an understanding that it's your responsibility to uphold what you value.

Often we view blessings as the end goal, the final reward after hardship. I challenge that perspective. The true blessing isn't just in achieving the desired outcome. It's in having the opportunity to pursue it in the first place. The opportunity to put in the work, to grow, and to evolve—that is the real gift. With that gift comes responsibility, which is the cornerstone of maintenance. It's what keeps you accountable for the opportunities and potential that come your way.

This brings us to a crucial question: Do you want to be happy? It seems like the answer is obvious, but there's a deeper layer to this question. Once you realize that happiness doesn't come from external circumstances but must be cultivated from within, you begin to see that happiness also requires maintenance. It's not something you can achieve once and be done with. Like any muscle, happiness requires consistent effort, care, and a commitment to yourself.

Happiness maintenance starts with choices—choosing what you allow into your life, setting boundaries, and knowing yourself well enough to make decisions that protect your peace. The responsibility for your own happiness rests squarely on your shoulders. This means not waiting for life to deliver happiness to you but cultivating it yourself intentionally through the decisions you make every day. This self-maintenance is essential for inner-peace and lasting fulfillment.

In conversations about success, we often neglect to discuss the hidden challenges that come with it. There's an illusion that once you achieve success, life becomes free of struggle. But that's far from the truth. Success brings its own set of challenges, and the ability to manage those stressors while maintaining your inner-peace is the true measure of success. The path to success is rarely smooth, but it's the continuous upkeep—the maintenance of your peace, your mindset, your resilience—that allows you to navigate those challenges with grace.

Wealth and happiness are often conflated, with society perpetuating the myth that having more money will make you more content. Anyone who has studied happiness or looked closely at the lives of millionaires knows that wealth doesn't guarantee inner-peace. In fact, the happiness of those who have fewer material riches but robust systems for valuing family, community, and communication often outshines that of the wealthy. It's not the accumulation of things but the maintenance of the important and often intangible aspects of life that determine one's sense of well-being.

Let's consider for a moment what it means to define a perfect day. What would that look like for you? Not in terms of grand gestures or major life events, but in the small, seemingly ordinary moments that contribute to your happiness. I challenge you to think about this because it's in the awareness of these small moments that we find lasting joy. A perfect day might not be free of challenges, but it's a day where you are present enough to acknowledge the good—the moments of connection, the peaceful pause in the middle of a busy day, the act of caring for yourself or others.

For me, the ability to slow down and appreciate the small things is a form of maintenance. "My awareness of these small things that make up a part of my happiness equation is essential. I slow down. I pay attention," I remind myself. It's this practice of paying attention, of being mindful of the fleeting but beautiful moments that sustains my happiness. Happiness isn't about waiting for everything to be perfect but rather recognizing the perfection that already exists in the present moment, no matter how small or temporary.

Maintenance is, at its core, a personal journey of stewardship. When you think of your peace and happiness as something that requires ongoing care, you realize that your body and mind are the tools through which you acquire both. Your body is not just something that moves you through the world. It is a vessel through which you generate joy, peace, and desired outcomes. By maintaining it through rest, nourishment, movement, and mindfulness, you give yourself the ability to interact with the world in a way that aligns with your highest intentions.

The process, when you break it down, is about stewardship of the body, the mind, and the spirit. It's the continuous cycle of becoming more aware of what you need to maintain your well-being, taking responsibility for those needs, and using the tools at your disposal to create a life of purpose and fulfillment. Maintenance isn't just about fixing things when they're broken. It's about preserving what works, improving what can be better, and acknowledging that everything—peace, happiness, and success—requires care to thrive.

How do we become better stewards of our lives? It starts with self-awareness. You must know yourself deeply—your needs, desires, weaknesses, and strengths. This awareness allows you to make informed decisions about how to maintain your inner-peace and happiness. Next comes responsibility. You can't rely on external forces to maintain these things for you. The world won't hand you peace or happiness. You must cultivate and protect both on your own. Finally, you must be efficient in the use of the tools you've been given. Whether those tools are physical (your body), emotional (your relationships), or spiritual (your values), they are there for you to use in service of creating the life you desire.

This cycle of self-awareness, responsibility, and efficient use of resources is what allows you to maintain the things that matter most. It's what allows you to not just achieve happiness, peace, or success but to keep it, nurture it, and let it grow. Maintenance may not be glamorous, but it is essential. It's the hidden work that goes into creating a life of fulfillment, a life of purpose, a life that you can truly call your own.

Living a life of awareness and personal growth isn't about arriving at some final destination. It's about embracing the journey itself—nurturing your peace, happiness, and sense of purpose in the everyday moments. The effort is ongoing, but so is the reward. With each passing day, every mindful step brings you closer to a life that authentically mirrors who you are and what matters most to you.

10

Self-Trust Through Realistic Understanding of Your Limits

Trust in yourself is not just about confidence, but about aligning with your true abilities and recognizing the unique strengths that reside within you.
Dr. Thurman E. Webb, Jr.

TRUSTING ONESELF IS NOT JUST ABOUT KNOWING WHO you are. It's about understanding who you are, the situations you're in, and how you respond within those situations. The more you explore and expand your lived experiences, the more information you gather—not just about **who** you are but also **when** you are. Self-trust isn't static. It's a dynamic process that evolves with each new experience, each lesson learned, and each reflection on past decisions.

This concept of self-trust may sound simple, but it's often one of the most challenging aspects of self-awareness. Humans, by nature, are wired to trust. We trust the pilot flying a plane or the driver next to us on a busy highway without much thought.

Yet when it comes to trusting our own instincts, our own inner-compass, we hesitate. Why is it that we find it easier to trust the competence of strangers than to trust our own feelings and decisions?

I believe the answer lies in the cumulative weight of our experiences. Past hurts, traumas, and disappointments create barriers to self-trust. We start to doubt ourselves, second-guessing our instincts because of the times we've been wrong or hurt. This erosion of trust within ourselves can lead to reliance on external validation where we allow others to dictate our choices, slowly silencing our inner-voice.

Self-trust is not a luxury but rather a necessity. It's what allows us to move through life confidently, to make decisions that align with who we are and navigate the complexity of relationships, careers, and challenges. Learning to trust yourself is a lifelong process, and it begins with understanding that trusting your instincts doesn't always mean you'll avoid failure. It does mean you'll be true to yourself.

THE TENDENCY TO TALK OURSELVES OUT OF INSTINCT

I've seen it time and again, both in my own life and in the lives of others. We have a gut feeling, a nagging sense that something is off, and yet we override it. We rationalize our way out of trusting ourselves, leaning on logic or societal expectations. A mentor once told me, "Trust that gut feeling once you know yourself." This wisdom became a guiding principle in my life.

I remember vividly a business deal I was involved in. Everything looked great on paper. The numbers aligned, the opportunities were there, but something deep within me didn't feel right. It wasn't logical, just a gut feeling. Part of me wanted to dismiss it. After all, everything seemed to be in order. But that small voice, that inner-knowing, kept whispering to me, "Be cautious." I trusted it and pulled back from the deal. A few months later, I found out that the company had collapsed due to internal mismanagement.

Had I ignored that instinct, I could have been caught in a financial disaster. That's the complexity surrounding self-trust. It doesn't always align with what's on the surface. Trusting yourself means listening when your instincts are screaming, even when the facts seem to point in a different direction.

Ignoring Feelings and the Consequences

One of the most dangerous traps we fall into is ignoring our feelings, especially when those feelings are trying to tell us something important. This is particularly true for young Black men, who are often conditioned to push through discomfort and override their emotions with adrenaline. In many communities, feelings such as fear or anxiety are seen as weaknesses and something to be suppressed or ignored. This suppression comes at a cost.

I've spoken with countless young men who misinterpret their anxiety as mere nervousness, forcing themselves to push through it, ignoring the signals their body and mind are sending. They find themselves in situations they could have avoided if they had just listened to their initial gut feeling. What they didn't realize was that anxiety, fear, or discomfort aren't just obstacles to overcome. They're cues, signals from the body that something isn't right.

It's critical that we learn to trust those signals, even when they don't make sense on the surface. Your intuition is your body's way of processing information that your conscious mind might not yet fully understand. It's that sense of discomfort that tells you to step away from a situation, or that feeling of calm that tells you it's safe to proceed. Ignoring these feelings can lead to regret, poor decisions, and in some cases, danger.

BOUNDARIES, "NO," AND PERSONAL AGENCY

One of the most important aspects of trusting yourself is learning to say "No" and believing it is a complete sentence. Many of us feel compelled to justify our boundaries, to explain why we're saying no, or to seek permission for our own decisions. Personal agency means recognizing that you are in control of your life, and you don't need external validation to stand by your choices.

For example, there was a time in my life when I would overexplain myself whenever I said no to someone. I felt like I owed them an explanation, like I needed their approval to assert my boundaries. As I grew in self-awareness, I realized that trusting myself meant understanding that my feelings and decisions are valid, period, no explanation required.

This became especially important in situations involving potential danger. Sometimes, your gut will tell you to say no or walk away without a clear reason why. Maybe the person or situation seems perfectly fine on the surface, but something inside you is saying otherwise. Trust that feeling. It's better to say no and be wrong than to ignore it and face consequences later.

This is particularly vital for young Black men, who often face mistreatment in everyday situations. They're frequently taught to "push through," to "not make waves," or to "be tough" in the face of adversity. But real courage lies in trusting yourself enough to remove yourself from harmful situations. It's about recognizing when your feelings are warning you and having the strength to listen to them.

HISTORICAL TRUST AND THE INSTINCT FOR SURVIVAL

There's a long history in our culture of needing to trust our instincts, even in situations where outward appearances seemed safe. Our ancestors often had to rely on their gut feelings to navigate a world filled with danger, whether it was the false kindness of an oppressor or the hidden threat behind a smile. That instinct, that ability to trust what you feel even when there's no evidence to support it, has been passed down through generations.

Trusting your feelings isn't just about avoiding danger. It's also about understanding the fullness of your humanity. Feelings are not obstacles to success, nor are they distractions from rational thought. They are a fundamental part of the human experience, offering insight and guiding our decisions. Learning to trust those feelings is not just an act of self-preservation but self-respect.

EMBRACING SELF-TRUST IN A NOISY WORLD

In today's world, external influences are louder than ever. Social media, societal pressures, and the constant influx of opinions can drown out your inner-voice. This is why it's crucial to work toward an accurate interpretation of your feelings. The more you understand yourself, the easier it becomes to differentiate between genuine intuition and external noise.

Self-trust requires reflection and quiet. It's about listening to yourself even when the world is telling you to doubt, to explain, or to justify. When you embrace self-trust, you begin to rely on your own inner-compass to guide you through life rather than waiting for external validation or approval.

Trusting yourself means being realistic about your limitations and capabilities. It means acknowledging when you don't have all the answers and being okay with that. It means being willing to make decisions that may not make sense to others but resonate deeply with you.

The Takeaway: Trust as the Foundation of Growth

Trusting yourself is not just about making the right decisions. It's about embracing the complexity of human intuition and learning to validate your own experiences. In a world that often encourages conformity and external validation, self-trust becomes an act of liberation. It empowers you to navigate your path authentically, to set boundaries, and to make decisions from a place of deep self-awareness.

To trust yourself is to trust the process of growth, knowing that each experience—whether it leads to success or failure—will bring you closer to understanding who you are and how you move through the world.

Debriefing

PART I OF *BE STILL, SAY LESS* FOCUSED ON THEMES OF SELF-awareness, personal growth, and resilience. It explored the interconnectedness of time, intention, and impact, emphasizing the importance of intentional living. The text delved into concepts such as responding versus reacting, the power of perspective, and the necessity of addressing trauma for personal growth. It also highlighted the significance of truth, accountability, critical thinking, and courage in building inner-resilience.

KEY THEMES

- **Time and Intention:** Time is a valuable, finite resource that should be used intentionally to create impact. Intentions must be followed by well-timed actions.
- **Self-Awareness:** Understanding oneself–including strengths, weaknesses, and emotional triggers–is crucial for personal growth. Self-discovery can be painful but leads to resilience.
- **Responding vs. Reacting:** Responding involves

thoughtful consideration, while reacting is often driven by emotions. Mastering the ability to respond with intention is essential.

- **Perspective:** Perspective shapes our experience of the world and influences personal growth. A positive perspective fuels resilience, while a negative one can hinder progress.
- **Trauma and Healing:** Trauma must be addressed and accepted rather than suppressed or ignored. Acceptance is the foundation of personal growth and healing.
- **Truth, Accountability, and Critical Thinking:** These elements are crucial for personal growth, self-awareness, and authentic leadership. Accountability requires honesty and taking responsibility for one's actions.
- **Courage and Inner-Resilience:** True courage comes from self-awareness and an inward journey. It involves valuing oneself and standing in one's truth.

AFFIRMATION

I embrace self-awareness and personal growth, knowing that resilience comes from within.

SELF-REFLECTION

Part I invites us to take a deeper look at our inner worlds by exploring the themes of time, perspective, and personal resilience. It challenges us to move beyond surface-level thinking and habitual responses, encouraging us to evaluate how we manage our time, how our perspectives shape our experiences, and how we cultivate the resilience necessary to navigate life's challenges. Rather than offering quick fixes or surface solutions, this section provides a framework for internal clarity—rooted in self-awareness, intentionality, and emotional strength. Take a moment to process the themes explored in Part I. Reflect on the following questions.

Time and Intentionality:
- Am I truly intentional with how I spend my time?
- Where do I find myself wasting time on distractions?
- How can I better align my actions with my intentions?
- Consider specific examples of how you currently use your time and how you *want* to use your time.

Responding vs. Reacting:
- Do I tend to react emotionally or respond thoughtfully in challenging situations?
- Can I recall a recent instance where I reacted instead of responded?
- What could I have done differently?
- What triggers my reactions?
- How can I cultivate more thoughtful response?

Perspective:
- How does my perspective influence my daily life?
- Do I tend to see things positively or negatively?
- What stories do I tell myself that shape my perspective?
- How can I shift my perspective to be more positive and empowering?
- Consider situations where your perspective may have limited you.

Trauma and Healing:
- How have past traumas shaped who I am today?
- Am I actively addressing and healing from past wounds, or am I avoiding them?
- What steps can I take to embrace and heal from my trauma?
- What does acceptance mean to me in this context?

Truth and Accountability:
- Am I honest with myself and others?
- Do I take full accountability for my actions?
- Where might I be avoiding accountability?
- In what areas of my life am I most truthful?
- Where am I least truthful?

Courage and Resilience:
- How do I define courage?
- Do I feel I possess inner resilience?
- When have I demonstrated courage in my life?
- How can I further develop my inner resilience?

Acceptance and Vulnerability:
- Am I able to accept myself and others without judgment or illusion?
- Where do I struggle with acceptance?
- How comfortable am I with being vulnerable?
- What benefits or discomforts do I associate with vulnerability?

Personal Growth:
- How committed am I to personal growth?
- What steps am I currently taking to grow?

- What areas of growth do I want to focus on?
- What obstacles do I perceive to my growth?

Impact:
- What kind of impact do I want to have on the world?
- Are my current actions aligned with this desired impact?
- What steps can I take to create more meaningful impact?

Overall:
- What key insights have I gained from Part 1?
- How can I apply these insights to my life moving forward?
- What action steps will I take to implement what I have learned?

Journaling on these questions can provide valuable insights into your current state and help you identify areas for growth and change. Be honest and compassionate with yourself during this reflection process.

Part II
Cultivating Stillness:

The Power of Connection, Awareness, and Intentionality

In this next section of our journey, we'll take a look at the pillars that shape the essence of who we are as a person. Within the realm of personal growth and fulfillment, we find ourselves traversing through 10 pillars that illuminate the path to a more meaningful and enriching life. These pillars serve as beacons, each casting a unique light on crucial aspects of our inner and outer worlds. From the warmth of friendship to the courage of dreaming big, from the tranquility of maintaining peace to the audacity of thinking differently, these pillars invite us to explore the depths of our humanity. Join us on this transformative journey as we delve into the profound wisdom encapsulated in the 10 pillars, unlocking the secrets to a life well-lived.

1

Curating Connections: Harnessing the Power of Relationships

> *If your awareness surpasses that of everyone else in the room, it's time to seek a new environment where your understanding can be challenged and expanded.*
> Dr. Thurman E. Webb, Jr.

"Watch the company you keep." You've probably heard that phrase at least once in your life from a parent, grandparent, or maybe even a wise mentor. The company you surround yourself with can make or break you. In his book *The Memo*, John Bryant points out that if you show him nine graduates, he'll show you the 10th graduate. If you show him nine thieves, he'll show you the 10th thief. This idea is simple but powerful. The people you surround yourself with influence your direction in life. Their values, attitudes, and actions become contagious, for better or worse. Hang out with a group of ambitious individuals, and chances are you'll find yourself striving for more. Hang out with people stuck in toxic cycles, and you might end up in the same rut.

What does this truth mean for increasing awareness? It means that your journey toward self-awareness is deeply intertwined with the company you keep. The people around you act as mirrors, reflecting parts of yourself that you might not see. They influence how you see yourself, what you believe is possible, and even how you think. If you want to grow into a more aware and authentic version of yourself, you need to surround yourself with people who not only reflect your values but also challenge you to be better.

DISCERNING AUTHENTICITY THROUGH SELF-AWARENESS

One of the first steps in increasing your awareness is learning how to discern who is truly in your corner. Your self-awareness helps you filter out the people who drain your energy or, worse, derail your personal growth. How can you know who these people are if you're not deeply connected to your own values and sense of purpose?

Self-awareness is your inner-compass. It guides you through the maze of relationships and helps you recognize when someone's energy aligns—or doesn't—with the person you're striving to become. For example, I had a close friend who fulfilled the hoop dreams of every young boy from the hood. He made it to the league. Of course, he enjoyed himself and made every mistake you'd expect a young Black man who became a millionaire overnight to make. However, after a few years passed, he stepped away from the NBA lifestyle. He was caught up in a whirlwind of fame, money, and superficial relationships. It wasn't until someone outside that world pointed out how disconnected he had become from his true self that he could see the impact his circle was having on him. Self-awareness doesn't just help you know yourself better. It also empowers you to see others more clearly. You start recognizing the subtle cues that tell you whether a person is building you up or pulling you down.

When you're aware of your own values and goals, you naturally begin to surround yourself with people who reflect those ideals. You stop settling for surface-level connections. Instead, you seek out those who challenge you to grow, who keep you accountable, and who share in your vision for personal and mutual development.

PRACTICES THAT FOSTER MUTUAL GROWTH

A significant aspect of increasing awareness is not just surrounding yourself with good-hearted people, but also committing to growth for yourself and those around you. It's important to adopt practices and mindsets that encourage continuous growth, both individually and within your circle. Consider the iron-sharpens-iron mentality. When you surround yourself with others who are equally motivated to grow, you push each other forward.

This doesn't mean you'll always agree or have smooth sailing. In fact, disagreements and challenges are inevitable but necessary. True growth often comes from the tension between who you are now and who you could become. Sometimes the people in your circle will call you out. They'll see the metaphorical "kick me" sign on your back that you might not notice. While their feedback might sting at first, it's crucial to your growth.

I remember a time when I thought I had it all figured out. I was living a fast-paced lifestyle, surrounded by people who, on the surface, seemed successful. When a friend pulled me aside and pointed out how far I had strayed from my core values, it forced me to reflect. At first, I resisted. Who were they to question me? As I sat with their words, I realized they were right. That moment of discomfort led to one of the most significant growth spurts in my life.

The people you trust to give you honest feedback are the ones who contribute to your personal and relational growth. They aren't afraid to hold a mirror up to you, showing you the parts of yourself that are out of alignment with your goals. This is why it's so important to surround yourself with people who are not just authentic but also growth-oriented. They'll challenge you in ways that superficial connections never will.

THE ROLE OF VULNERABILITY IN BUILDING AUTHENTIC RELATIONSHIPS

Vulnerability is often seen as a weakness but in truth, it's one of the greatest strengths you can bring into your relationships. Being vulnerable means showing up as your true self, flaws and all, and allowing others to do the same. When you're open about your struggles, fears, and ambitions, you create space for deeper, more authentic connections.

In my experience, vulnerability has been the key to forming relationships with people who are genuinely good-hearted and motivated to grow. The more open I've been, the more I've attracted people who resonate with that honesty. It's through vulnerability that you find your tribe—the people who will stick by you when things get tough, who will challenge you when you need it and celebrate your victories, no matter how small.

The real estate agent I met in Indiana had it right when she asked me if my friend and I had ever fought. At the time, I didn't understand what she was getting at. Now I know that real relationships aren't built on a lack of conflict but rather the ability to navigate those conflicts with honesty and integrity. The people who can see you at your worst and still believe in your best are the ones worth keeping around.

Increasing your awareness is never a solitary path. It's woven into the connections you form with the people around you, those who share your values, challenge you to grow, and accept you in your most vulnerable moments. These individuals help reveal your truest self, encouraging you to move beyond the image you present to the world. With their support, you'll navigate to the heart of your story and lead a more meaningful and authentic life.

2

The Power of Kindness: Fueling Personal Growth and Expanding Awareness

> *Kindness transcends actions. It is a reflection of your*
> *essence and the awareness you bring to every moment.*
> Dr. Thurman E. Webb, Jr.

"KINDNESS DOESN'T COST YOU ANYTHING" IS A PHRASE I often share. Behind that simple truth lies a deep well of meaning. I've learned in my own life that kindness, while free in its delivery, is priceless in its impact, especially on personal growth and awareness. It's not just about being nice to others or doing good deeds. It's about embodying kindness as a way of being, as a principle that influences how we engage with the world and most importantly, how we treat ourselves.

I've done a lot of work on myself over the years. I still take self-inventory every single day, sometimes multiple times a day. I ask myself the same set of questions inspired by Frantz Fanon:

Who am I? Am I who I say I am? Am I all I ought to be? These questions keep me in check, in alignment with my values, honest about the progress I've made, and the areas where I still need work. They push me to go beyond surface-level niceness and dig deeper into a more profound kindness, one that starts from within.

KINDNESS AS A REFLECTION OF SELF-INVENTORY

Through my daily self-inventory, I've come to realize that I am kind, but I'm not always nice. This may sound like a contradiction, but it's an important distinction. I'll give you the shirt off my back if you need it, but I'll also ask you why you don't have one. That's not cruelty. It's holding you accountable for your growth. My kindness isn't about making people comfortable but rather about pushing them to be better. This approach to kindness comes from my own upbringing.

Growing up on the east side of Nashville in a community where scarcity was the norm, my mother always emphasized the importance of kindness. Even when we had very little, she would say, "One day, you'll have your own and when you do, operate with kindness." It was never just about being nice to others. It was about recognizing that everyone and everything has a right to exist, even if they're not on your same path. She taught me that kindness was a way to coexist with others, not necessarily to engage or align with everyone but to respect their right to be.

Operating with kindness requires a balance of understanding and boundaries. It's knowing when to help and when to step back. It's offering support but also challenging people to do better for themselves. This type of kindness is not always easy or comfortable, but it's necessary for growth both for yourself and those around you.

KINDNESS AS A PATH TO HEALING

My mother's emphasis on kindness didn't just come from a place of moral duty. It was deeply tied to her own healing. She had seen firsthand how negativity and a lack of compassion had consumed and derailed so many people who shared our circumstances. She was used to seeing people lose hope after an eviction notice was taped to their door. Some people try harder, but in my experience I've seen more people give up. When despair is everywhere and the world you know only exists between 69th Street and 71st Place, you want to escape. For a lot of our neighbors, that escape came from drugs. Thankfully, for mom, kindness was the antidote to the generational curses that plagued our family. It was her way of ensuring that we didn't become victims of our environment and that we didn't internalize the struggles we faced as children of poverty.

Kindness, in this context, wasn't about being passive or submissive. It was a form of resistance. It was about not letting the world harden you, about not becoming the very thing you despised. In a world that often teaches us that to overcome the bully we must become the bully, kindness goes against the grain. Embracing it helps you maintain your sense of self and your humanity, even in the face of adversity.

This lesson has stayed with me throughout my life. Kindness, I've found, is necessary for entering into therapeutic spaces. It's the key to healing, both for yourself and for others. Without kindness, it's impossible to create a space where real healing can happen. Healing is essential for growth. You can't grow if you're constantly fighting battles that leave you scarred and hardened. Kindness allows you to soften, be vulnerable, and heal from the inside out.

KINDNESS AS A WAY OF BEING

One of the reasons people struggle with kindness is because they reduce it to something you do instead of something you are. Kindness isn't about a set of actions but rather is a state of being. It's about showing up in the world with a mindset that values connection, empathy, and respect. It's about seeing others as worthy of kindness, even when they may not deserve it, and even when it's hard. More importantly, it's about showing that same kindness to yourself.

This is where many people stumble, myself included. We're often harder on ourselves than we are on others. We expect perfection and when we fall short, we judge ourselves harshly. I've seen it in people I've worked with over the years, individuals who believe in divine forgiveness yet struggle to forgive themselves. They carry shame and guilt like a heavy cloak, unable to shed it, even when they know they've been forgiven by their higher power.

Why is it so hard to show ourselves the same kindness we extend to others? I believe it's because we're so deeply entrenched in self-deception. We convince ourselves that we're not worthy of the same mercy we grant to others, but kindness toward yourself is essential for growth. It allows you to acknowledge your mistakes, learn from them, and move forward without being weighed down by guilt or shame. When you can show yourself kindness, you open the door to genuine self-love, and that's where real transformation begins.

DR. THURMAN E. WEBB, JR.

THE ROLE OF KINDNESS IN ACCOUNTABILITY

Kindness doesn't mean letting yourself or others off the hook. It's not about ignoring mistakes or excusing bad behavior. In fact, kindness often requires accountability. Early in my career, I had a moment that exemplified this perfectly. I was working on a project with a young woman who wanted to partner with an NBA player I was associated with. I had gone out partying the night before, and the next morning, still a little buzzed, I sent her a rough draft of our proposal. She called me back and went off. She didn't hold back in telling me that what I had sent was absolute garbage and that if this was my best effort, we wouldn't be working together again.

At first, I was defensive. Who did she think she was to talk to me like that? After some reflection and a little self-inventory, I realized she was right. I hadn't given my best effort, and she had every right to call me out on it. That experience was a turning point for me. From that moment on, I vowed that no one would ever have the opportunity to question my professionalism again. Her harsh words were actually an act of kindness. She held me accountable because she knew I could do better.

Kindness, when done right, doesn't shy away from tough conversations. It's about helping people grow, even if that means making them uncomfortable. It's about holding yourself and others to a higher standard not out of judgment but a desire to see everyone around you succeed. It's the type of kindness that says, "I believe in you, and I'm not going to let you settle for less than you're capable of achieving."

SELF-INVENTORY AND THE EVOLUTION OF KINDNESS

Part of my daily self-inventory is checking in on how I'm evolving, both in terms of my actions and my mindset. I believe that if you're the same person every day, that's a problem. I realize there is some merit in remaining true to yourself and not wavering from your values, but remaining the same means you haven't learned anything new, and you're not growing. Kindness, like everything else, needs to be examined regularly. Are you operating from a place of genuine kindness, or are you just going through the motions? Are you being kind to yourself, or are you still carrying the weight of past mistakes and failures?

Self-inventory isn't just about internal reflection. It's about how you engage with the world. It's about recognizing the impact you have on others and adjusting your actions accordingly. Kindness, when practiced consistently, becomes a way of life. It's no longer something you do but rather who you are.

Like anything else, kindness needs to be nurtured. You need to take stock of where you are, how you're evolving, and whether you're truly living up to your potential. That's why I believe in the power of self-inventory. It allows me to see where I'm making progress and where I need to improve, which is the key to personal growth. It's not about being perfect. It's about making small, incremental improvements every day.

KINDNESS AS A CATALYST FOR GROWTH

At the end of the day, kindness is more than just a virtue. It's a catalyst for personal growth and self-awareness. It's through kindness that we heal, hold ourselves accountable, and grow into the best versions of ourselves. True kindness starts from within. It's about being kind to yourself first, showing yourself the grace and compassion you need to grow. Once you've mastered that, it naturally extends to others.

Kindness doesn't cost you anything, but its value is immeasurable. It's the foundation of personal growth, the key to healing, and the pathway to a more aware and authentic life. When you operate from a place of kindness toward yourself and others, you create a ripple effect that not only changes your life but the lives of everyone around you. In the end, that is the true power of kindness.

3

Turning Dreams into Reality: The Journey of Creation

> *Your dreams can come true, but first you have to wake up*
> *and do the work to make them a reality.*
> Dr. Thurman E. Webb, Jr.

GETTING INTO A LEARNING MINDSET IS LIKE GIVING BIRTH to new ideas. The ability to create is inherent in all of us, but not everyone taps into it. I've met countless people—many of them brilliant and full of potential—who seem to have lost their spark. They've stopped practicing creation in their careers, personal lives, or even in how they approach relationships. There is artistry in every profession and every life. Whether you're an engineer, a therapist, or a teacher, there's opportunity to express your unique flair. What sets you apart is your ability to create something new that only you can bring to life.

Creating is about leaving your mark on this world and involves being in a constant state of learning and curiosity. Embracing a learning mindset is crucial but it's not always easy, especially in a society that pressures people—particularly Black men—to always appear knowledgeable and competent. It can become incredibly challenging to be okay with not knowing. The expectation is that you have the answers and are always on top of things. What if we flip that narrative? What if the power lies in admitting that you don't know everything and that being a beginner is not only okay, but is actually where real creation starts?

It's that beginner's mindset that made you an expert in the first place. Think about the last time you were truly curious about something. Maybe you didn't know the first thing about it, but that didn't stop you from diving in and learning everything you could. That hunger for knowledge propelled you forward and before you knew it, you were an expert. The same is true for every great idea or dream. It starts with being willing to admit to not knowing and then committing to learning as much as you can.

When I think back to my own life, I see this process over and over again. After I earned my doctorate degree, I realized something significant: I hadn't created a vision for what came next. I had done the impossible, something that no one in my family had ever done. I was Dr. Thurman E. Webb, Jr., standing there with a title that many people would see as the pinnacle of success. What no one told me was that after you reach the top of the mountain, you still have to figure out where to go. I hadn't thought past the doctorate because I had no idea how I would get there in the first place. I didn't plan on becoming a doctor. It wasn't even a dream of mine at the beginning but rather my mother's vision.

I remember vividly the sacrifices my mother made after she divorced my father when I was just two years old. She created a life for us that was filled with possibilities, even though we had very little. She had a vision for me when I didn't have one for myself. She pushed me to think beyond our circumstances, to understand that reality could be molded by our actions, our thoughts, and our dreams.

As a child, I didn't realize how much of an influence she had on me. I knew that going to college seemed impossible. We couldn't afford it, and no one in our family had ever been to college. But my mother was undeterred. She knew about grants and scholarships, and she made a plan for me to attend Tennessee State University. Together, we created a pathway to college. When I got there, I realized I hadn't created a plan to finish.

I was just there, floating along, unsure of my purpose. That's when I met Dr. Peter Millet, a professor who helped me understand who I was. He helped me see my potential and piqued my interest in psychology and counseling. More importantly, he helped me create a plan to get out of college versus become another dropout and sad statistic. For the first time, I began to envision something bigger for myself.

After I graduated, I didn't have a plan to pursue a doctorate. That was my mother's dream. I still remember the day she was diagnosed with cancer. We were sitting together, and I looked deeply into her eyes and thought about all the things she had done for me throughout my life and all the things she wanted me to be. In that moment, her dream became my dream.

I pursued my doctorate, not because it was something I had always wanted, but because I saw how much it meant to her. When I achieved it, I stood in a space that wasn't really mine. It wasn't until after I had reached that milestone that I realized I hadn't created a vision for what came next.

This is where so many people get stuck. They reach their goals, but then what? The truth is, creating a vision for your life doesn't end when you achieve something great. It's a continual process, one that requires you to keep dreaming, keep creating, and keep learning.

THE IMPORTANCE OF REIMAGINING YOUR LIFE

Creating new dreams means you have to shed old identities. After I earned my doctorate, I had to let go of the idea that I had "made it." I had to realize that the title didn't define me, and I wasn't just a product of my achievements. This is something many people struggle with as well, especially in communities where stability and productivity are seen as the ultimate goals. For many of us, the question isn't whether we're happy but whether we're doing enough to maintain that stability.

True fulfillment isn't about what you've done but rather how you feel about who you are. I had to learn to appreciate myself without constantly seeking recognition. After all, accolades fade. You can only ride the wave of one success for so long before it disappears, leaving you feeling empty if you've placed all your worth in that achievement.

I see this in students all the time. They chase the next award, the next honor, the next promotion, thinking that will be the accomplishment that fulfills them. The reality is, success is fleeting. What really matters is cultivating an appreciation for who you are, not just what you do. This takes time and requires self-reflection—a willingness to sit with yourself and ask the hard questions: **Who am I beyond my accomplishments? What makes me truly happy?**

THE POWER OF SOLITUDE AND SELF-REFLECTION

One of the most important things I've learned is the value of solitude. In a world that rewards constant productivity and busyness, taking time to be alone with your thoughts feels counterintuitive. But it's essential for personal growth. It's in those quiet moments of reflection that you begin to understand what truly matters to you. It's where you cultivate self-awareness and gain clarity about your dreams and aspirations.

When I was younger, I used to chase after recognition. I wanted people to notice me, to see that I was doing something important. The more I pursued external validation, the more I realized how empty it left me. True fulfillment comes from within and appreciating the journey, not just the destination.

Taking time to reflect allows you to process your experiences, to make sense of your emotions, and to chart a path forward that's aligned with your true self. This is especially important when you're in the process of creating something new, whether it's a career, a relationship, or a chapter in your life. If you don't take the time to reflect, you run the risk of simply repeating old patterns and staying stuck in the same place.

NURTURING YOUR DREAMS THROUGH EMPATHY AND APPRECIATION

As I've grown older, I've learned that creating and making your dreams come true isn't just about setting goals and achieving them. It's about nurturing those dreams with empathy and appreciation—empathy for yourself when things don't go as planned and appreciation for the process of learning and growing along the way.

There's a difference between recognition and appreciation. Recognition is about what you do. It's the awards, the praise, the acknowledgment of your achievements. Appreciation, on the other hand, is about who you are. It's about valuing yourself and others for their inherent worth, not just for what they produce.

When you approach your dreams from a place of appreciation, you allow yourself the grace to make mistakes, to pivot when necessary, and to grow without the constant pressure of needing to be perfect. You start to see your journey not as a series of achievements to be checked off a list but as a continuous process of learning and becoming.

This shift in mindset has made all the difference in my life. I no longer measure my worth by my accomplishments but by how I feel about the person I'm becoming. In the end, that is what creating your dreams is really about. It's about constantly evolving, learning, and creating a vision for your life that aligns with who you truly are.

4

Breaking Boundaries: Expanding Awareness Beyond Limiting Beliefs

> *Rather than merely thinking outside the box, expand*
> *your awareness to realize that the box itself is an illusion.*
> Deepak Chopra

"Rather than merely thinking outside the box, expand your awareness to realize that the box itself is an illusion," said Deepak Chopra. This idea has stayed with me for years, slowly unraveling layers of understanding about how we navigate life. At first, the phrase seemed simple—just another way of encouraging creativity. The more I've reflected, the more profound it became. The "box," as I've come to understand, is not just a metaphor for limitations imposed on us by society or circumstance. It's the mental structures we create ourselves. It's the prison of our own thoughts, beliefs, and assumptions—the invisible walls that keep us trapped in narrow perspectives. Often, we don't even realize we're stuck inside.

The mind is a powerful thing. It creates stories, narratives, and explanations for everything we experience. But sometimes, those stories are just that—stories. We get so lost in our own thoughts that we start believing each one is rational and every idea is universally applicable. We assume everyone would act the same way, think the same way, and feel the same way if they were in our shoes. The reality, though, is far more nuanced.

Our thoughts often drift toward pleasure, comfort, and what feels right in the moment. The brain is wired to avoid discomfort and so, we gravitate toward ideas and actions that minimize pain or challenge. Here's the danger: Just because something feels right doesn't make it right. Just because a thought seems logical doesn't mean it accounts for all the variables. When we stay inside our mental box, we risk doing the right thing at the wrong time or worse, doing the wrong thing altogether because we failed to see beyond our own assumptions.

QUESTIONING OUR OWN THOUGHTS

I've often found myself falling into the trap of believing that the way I see the world is the way everyone else should. When you think this way long enough, it's easy to dismiss other perspectives. You think, "Why can't they just see things the way I do?" It's not that simple. People come from different experiences, backgrounds, and contexts. Their perspectives are shaped by things we may never fully understand.

A real-life example of this came to me during a conference I attended a few years ago. I was seated at a table with three women, each of different ethnicities. The conversation turned to the topic of hiring practices in the sports industry, particularly when it came to female coaches hiring male assistants. Collectively, these women had come to the conclusion that no female coach should hire a male assistant because he would inevitably try to dominate the room or take over the job. I remember sitting there, nodding along at first, until I realized something didn't feel right about their conclusion.

It struck me how easily we can fall into the trap of believing that our internal thoughts and biases are universal truths. The women's conclusion was based on their personal experiences, but it had become a blanket rule in their minds. In that moment, I had to remind myself and them that not every man is the same, just as not every woman is the same. To assume otherwise was to perpetuate a harmful stereotype, one that could limit opportunities for good people. It was a reminder that just because a thought feels right doesn't make it true. We have to challenge ourselves and each other to question internal narratives, especially when they come packaged as absolutes.

The same kind of thinking led to some of the darkest moments in our history. During post-slavery Reconstruction, the assumption that Black men were inherently dangerous or incapable of integrating into society led to countless lynchings and acts of violence. That same closed-mindedness persists today, just in different forms. When we fail to expand our awareness and realize the limitations of our own thoughts, we contribute to the very problems we think we're trying to solve.

THE IMPORTANCE OF DIVERSE PERSPECTIVES

One of the greatest lessons I've learned is that we shouldn't believe everything we think. It's easy to surround ourselves with people who think and act like us or share our worldview. When everyone in your circle thinks the same, you're at risk of living in an echo chamber. You need diversity of thought. You need people who challenge you by bringing perspectives you might never have considered.

In relationships, this is especially important. I've heard people say, "There are no good men (or women) out there," as though the entire dating pool is to blame for their bad experiences. It's an easy conclusion to draw when you're stuck inside your own head, but it's as flawed as blaming fruit for not being sweet when you don't know how to pick a ripened piece. Just because you've chosen poorly in the past doesn't mean no good options exist. Sometimes, you need to refine your ability to choose, which requires stepping outside your comfort zone and exposing yourself to new experiences and perspectives.

This process of getting out of your head and out of your own way is like peeling back layers. It requires openness, vulnerability, and a willingness to be wrong. It also requires engaging with people you trust, people who will call you out when you're stuck in your own narrative. These are the people who help you refine your thoughts, who add layers of perspective to your thinking. They expand your awareness, helping you see the bigger picture.

THE LIMITS OF OUR THINKING

I often tell people that when you talk to someone long enough, you can tell what they read or if they read at all. People who expose themselves to diverse sources of information tend to have a broader vocabulary and a wider perspective. On the other hand, those who rely on a single source tend to repeat themselves, cycling through the same ideas over and over. It's like eating the same meal every day. Eventually, you get tired of it. Life is not about perpetually consuming the same information. It's about constantly taking in new ideas, letting them mingle with your existing thoughts to create new insights.

This does not mean you have to change your beliefs every time you encounter a new idea. It's not about abandoning who you are. It's about realizing that growth happens when you allow yourself to be challenged. The box—the mental construct we live inside—is an illusion. It's not real. The boundaries we think exist are only there because we've put them there. When you expand your awareness, when you engage with new perspectives, you start to see that there's no box at all. There's only the vast, limitless potential of what you can learn and create.

EXPANDING AWARENESS IN EVERYDAY LIFE

Expanding awareness isn't a one-time event but rather a continual practice that happens in everyday moments. We often think of awakening as this grand, transformative experience but the truth is, it often begins in the quieter spaces of daily existence. Awareness starts with noticing the small things—the stories we tell ourselves, the judgments we make, and the patterns we fall into. It's in these moments that we realize how much of our lives we spend inside the boxes we've constructed for ourselves.

One quote that has deeply resonated with me is from the great African American writer Audre Lorde, who said, "Your silence will not protect you." This statement is a profound reminder that when we remain silent about our inner-thoughts and the illusions we build, we do nothing to challenge them. Expanding awareness requires us to break that silence, not just outwardly but inwardly as well. It demands that we question the very narratives that run on a loop in our minds. Silence and avoidance may feel comfortable, but they ultimately keep us locked inside our illusions.

For years, I thought I had everything figured out. I had earned my doctorate, I was pursuing my career, and I was hitting all the milestones that society deemed an indication of success. But beneath the surface, there was a quiet discomfort I didn't want to acknowledge. It took time and a willingness to break my internal silence to realize that I had been living according to someone else's script. I had to ask myself difficult questions: What do I really want? What truly matters to me?

This self-inquiry, inspired by Lorde's push to speak the truth, led me to see that my ambitions, while worthy, were often driven by external validation. I was checking boxes, but none of them were mine. Expanding awareness in this way involves courage to speak up, even to yourself, and admit that you've been trapped by illusions of success, expectations, or identity.

African American author Bell Hooks also sheds light on this idea of awareness in everyday life. She wrote, "The moment we choose to love, we begin to move against domination, against oppression. The moment we choose to love, we begin to move toward freedom." To expand awareness is, in many ways, an act of love for yourself, for truth, and for possibility. It's about choosing to break free from the mental cages that dominate our thinking. It's about loving yourself enough to ask, "Am I truly free in my thoughts, or am I confined by old beliefs?" This kind of awareness creates space for new ideas, dreams, and possibilities to flourish.

BE STILL, SAY LESS

THE CHALLENGE OF COLLECTIVE THINKING

While expanding our personal awareness is essential, the challenge of collective thinking can make this journey even more complex. On one hand, we are social beings, naturally inclined to align with the thoughts, beliefs, and values of the groups we belong to. But what happens when the collective mindset limits rather than liberates? What do we do when the groupthink keeps us in a narrow box where creativity, individuality, and authentic expression are stifled?

Toni Morrison once said, "If you want to fly, you have to give up the things that weigh you down." In the context of collective thinking, this quote takes on a powerful meaning. To soar into new levels of awareness, we must be willing to let go of the comfort of conformity. Groupthink can often weigh us down, trapping us in a cycle where we're afraid to challenge the consensus or voice a different perspective. The weight of collective agreement can be a heavy burden, keeping us from expanding into new possibilities.

I've seen this in various professional and personal settings. In group dynamics, especially when everyone around you shares a similar perspective, it's easy to fall into the habit of thinking that what the group believes must be true. Just as I learned from the conversation with those women at the conference about hiring practices, collective thinking can reinforce harmful ideas when it goes unchallenged. It reminded me of Zora Neale Hurston's words: "If you are silent about your pain, they'll kill you and say you enjoyed it." Staying quiet in the face of limiting groupthink can be detrimental, not just to yourself but to others. It can reinforce the very systems of thought that hold us all back.

To rise above the limitations of collective thinking, we need to embrace a multiplicity of perspectives. We must engage in conversations with people who challenge us, who see the world differently, and who invite us to step out of the collective box. As we expand our awareness, we learn that true liberation comes not from agreeing with everyone but from standing in our truth even when it's uncomfortable. As Hurston implies, silence and conformity can be lethal, not just to our individual growth but to the collective potential we all share.

SEEING BEYOND THE BOX

Seeing beyond the box is about realizing that the limitations we perceive—whether in our thinking, our circumstances, or our relationships—are often illusions. They are constructs of our minds, shaped by past experiences, societal norms, and internalized beliefs. Once we recognize that the box is an illusion, we have the power to dissolve it.

In *Sister Outsider*, Audre Lorde wrote, "It is not our differences that divide us. It is our inability to recognize, accept, and celebrate those differences." This quote is a powerful reminder that much of what confines us is rooted in our failure to see beyond the surface. The box we live in often disguises itself as "the way things are." It is only when we expand our awareness that we begin to see that there is so much more outside of it.

When I reflect on my own life, I see how I've been trapped by invisible boxes built from societal expectations about success, identity, and what it means to be an African American man in this world. The more I engaged in self-inquiry, the more I realized that many of these beliefs were not mine. They were borrowed, inherited, and holding me back.

Hooks offers another profound insight: "To be truly visionary, we have to root our imagination in our concrete reality while simultaneously imagining possibilities beyond that reality." Seeing beyond the box is about understanding that while we live in a specific reality, we also have the ability to imagine something greater. It's about balancing the awareness of where we are with the vision of where we can go.

This kind of thinking expands awareness in a way that challenges us to question not only our own assumptions but also the assumptions of the world around us. It asks, "What if everything you believe is only a partial truth?" It encourages us to embrace a mindset that is constantly evolving, open to new perspectives, and willing to see the illusions for what they are—temporary constructs that can be reshaped or discarded altogether.

The box only exists as long as we believe in its boundaries. As we expand our awareness, we realize the limitations we once accepted are not set in stone. They're instead flexible, ready to be reshaped. The key lies in continuously questioning, learning, and imagining new possibilities. The box represents an illusion of helplessness. When we recognize this, we regain the power to shape our reality not just for ourselves but for the world around us. Breaking free from the box isn't just an act of personal liberation. It sparks collective freedom. By expanding our awareness, we open the door for others to do the same.

5

The Essence of Love: A Journey of Intentionality and Purpose

Embrace your unique self, for in a world of infinite possibilities, authenticity is your greatest asset.
Dr. Thurman E. Webb, Jr.

WE OFTEN SPEAK OF LOVE AS THOUGH IT IS AN effortless event, something that happens by accident like catching a breeze on a sunny day or stumbling upon a beautiful sunset. This serendipitous notion of love is romanticized everywhere—from novels to movies, to the carefully curated moments we see on social media. Love, in this narrative, is easy and magical, requiring little more than existing in the right place at the right time. But love in its true essence, the kind that endures and grows, is far from effortless. It requires intention, commitment, and the kind of hard work that most people shy away from.

James Baldwin, the celebrated African American writer, once wrote, "Love takes off the masks we fear we cannot live without and know we cannot live within." Baldwin's words capture the heart of what real love demands from us—vulnerability and honesty with others and ourselves. Love requires us to step out from behind the mask that we present to the world, the carefully curated version of ourselves that we think will protect us. The mask might help us avoid pain in the short term but in the long run, it keeps us from experiencing the deep, fulfilling love we crave. Real love, the kind that grows and lasts, begins when the mask comes off and our true selves emerge.

Much like tending a garden, love is something that must be cultivated intentionally. You can't simply plant a seed and hope that it will grow. It requires daily attention—watering, weeding, nurturing. You must show up for it even on the days when you don't feel like it. Just as a garden will wither without care, love will fade if left unattended. Love is consequently not simply a feeling but rather a commitment to showing up, being present, and doing the hard work of understanding another person while allowing them to understand you.

Here's the challenge: Love also opens us up to hurt. The possibility of pain, rejection, and disappointment becomes real the moment we decide to love someone. For many, this fear of potential hurt can be paralyzing. The thought of being vulnerable, of allowing someone else to see our flaws, is terrifying. In an effort to sidestep that anticipated pain, we make choices that ultimately lead us down a path of avoidance. We present a version of ourselves that we believe will be loved rather than allowing ourselves to be fully seen.

Ta-Nehisi Coates, another brilliant African American writer, captures the essence of this fear when he writes, "In America, it is traditional to destroy the Black body, its heritage." Coates' reflection on the historical destruction of Black bodies resonates beyond physical harm. It speaks to the emotional and psychological scars that come from living in a world where vulnerability is often met with violence or disdain. This history makes the risk of love feel even more dangerous for those who have experienced generational trauma. The stakes of being vulnerable, of loving and being loved, are higher when the world has so often treated vulnerability as weakness.

To protect ourselves, we put on masks. We show the world what we think it wants to see–the version of ourselves that is invulnerable, self-sufficient, and whole. As Baldwin reminds us, "Love takes off the masks." The mask may protect us from immediate pain, but it also keeps us from genuine connection. When we wear the mask, we prevent others from truly seeing us and in doing so, we also prevent ourselves from truly experiencing love. We forget that it's not our perfect selves that make us worthy of love, but our authentic selves–the messy, imperfect, and flawed individuals we are underneath the mask.

The idea that we must always present our best selves is reinforced by the world we live in. Social media, television, and societal expectations constantly remind us of our perceived inadequacies. Everywhere we look, we see images of perfection–perfect relationships, perfect bodies, perfect lives. It's no wonder that we feel the pressure to hide our true selves. As we strive to live up to these unrealistic standards, we lose sight of what truly matters. We forget that love is not about being perfect but rather about being real.

This aversion to vulnerability and allowing ourselves to be fully seen extends to the emotions we try to avoid, especially sadness. In a world that celebrates happiness and success, sadness is often viewed as something to be avoided at all costs. We are taught to chase pleasure and comfort while running from discomfort and pain. But Baldwin offers us another perspective on pain and sadness: "Not everything that is faced can be changed, but nothing can be changed until it is faced." Sadness, while uncomfortable, offers us an opportunity for introspection, for slowing down and recalibrating our lives.

Sadness forces us to pause and take stock of where we are. It encourages awareness, a genuine acknowledgment of what is happening both within and around us. Rather than something to be avoided, sadness can be a gift. It allows us to step back, reassess our lives, and realign our thoughts, actions, and words. True awareness, after all, is about alignment. It's about ensuring that what we think, what we say, and what we do are all in harmony. When things go astray, sadness often serves as a reminder that something needs to change.

In love, as in life, awareness is crucial. It's not enough to simply feel love or express it. We must also be aware of the ways in which our thoughts, actions, and words either nurture or harm that love. Are we showing up as our true selves, or are we hiding behind a mask? Are we allowing ourselves to be vulnerable, or are we guarding our hearts out of fear? Are we nurturing our relationships, or are we taking them for granted? These are the questions we must ask ourselves if we want to experience the fullness of love.

Baldwin also stated: "Love does not begin and end the way we seem to think it does. Love is a battle, love is a war; love is a growing up." These words remind us that love is not static. It is not a momentary feeling or a singular event. Love is a process, a continual unfolding that requires growth, both individually and together. It is a battle not against each other but against our own fears, insecurities, and resistance to vulnerability.

When we expand our understanding of love to include this intentionality, this willingness to grow and to be vulnerable, we begin to see that love is not about finding someone who makes us feel good all the time. It's about finding someone who is willing to walk with us through the uncomfortable moments, the difficult conversations, the hard truths. It's about committing to the process of growth–both our own and our partner's.

The challenge of love is that it requires us to face ourselves, to confront the parts of us that we would rather keep hidden. It is in that confrontation that true connection is born. When we take off the mask, when we allow ourselves to be seen, we open the door to a love that is deeper and more fulfilling than anything we could have imagined. We move beyond the surface, beyond the carefully curated image, and into something real.

Coates once wrote, "The struggle is really all I have for you because it is the only thing I can guarantee." Love too is a struggle, but it is a beautiful one. It is the kind of struggle that shapes us and teaches us what it means to be human. It is a battle, not against each other, but against the walls we build around our hearts. In that struggle and vulnerability, we find something truly worth fighting for.

Love isn't about avoiding pain or discomfort. It's about embracing life in all its fullness—the highs and lows, the joy and the sorrow, the growth and the challenges. True love demands showing up with intention and commitment, even when it feels difficult. It invites vulnerability, asking us to strip away the defenses that hide our true selves. Love isn't about perfection but rather revealing our authentic selves with all our complexity. It's in this raw openness, when we let ourselves be truly seen, that love deepens and the real journey begins.

6

From Complacency to Leadership: Stepping into Your Potential

I'm not a businessman. I'm a business, man.
Jay Z

WHEN I THINK BACK TO MY TRANSITION FROM complacency to leadership, it's clear that it was not a single, defining moment but rather a series of internal and external challenges that slowly reshaped my sense of purpose. Moving from a place of comfort to a position where others look to you for guidance isn't easy. The process is often uncomfortable and forces you to confront parts of yourself that you'd rather avoid. It's through these challenges that real growth happens and you begin to redefine not just your role as a leader but your understanding of what it means to show up authentically in the world.

INTERNAL AND EXTERNAL CHALLENGES: THE BATTLE WITHIN AND AROUND

Internally, one of the greatest challenges I faced was battling complacency. Once you've reached a certain level of success, it's easy to settle into a routine. I was eating comfortably, both literally and figuratively, and that comfort bred stagnation. The hunger that had driven me in my earlier years when I was still trying to prove myself had started to fade. I was no longer pushing myself to learn new things or take risks because, quite frankly, I didn't need to. I had achieved what many people would call success. But success, I learned, can be a trap. It can lull you into a false sense of security, making you believe that you've reached the pinnacle of your potential when in reality, there's always more to learn, more to achieve, more to give.

Externally, the environment around me also played a role in reinforcing that complacency. I had surrounded myself with people who were content with the status quo, people who were comfortable in their positions and didn't feel the need to grow or push themselves further. It's easy to fall in line with the people around you, to adopt their mindset, and to believe that where you are is good enough. But leadership isn't about being comfortable. It's about stepping into the unknown, taking risks, and pushing yourself—and those around you—beyond what you thought was possible.

Breaking free from that environment meant making deliberate choices to reconnect with the hunger that had once driven me. As I mentioned earlier, I chose not to move into an affluent neighborhood, even though I had the means to do so. Instead, I built my house in a place that would remind me of where I came from. Every day, as I drive past those Section 8 homes, I'm reminded of my past struggles, my literal and figurative hunger. That external reminder helped me reconnect with my internal drive, reminding me of the importance of staying grounded, empathetic, and always striving for more.

Overcoming these challenges reshaped my sense of purpose in profound ways. I began to see leadership not as a position of power or authority, but as a responsibility that required me to remain in a constant state of learning and growth. I realized that my purpose wasn't just to achieve personal success but to use my experiences, both the successes and the struggles, to guide others on their own journeys. Leadership, I learned, is about showing up every day with intention, about being willing to do the hard work of self-reflection and growth, and about helping others do the same.

EVOLVING VISION OF LEADERSHIP: FROM STATUS QUO TO RESPONSIBILITY

As I moved from being comfortable with the status quo to actively taking responsibility for guiding others, my vision of leadership began to evolve. Early on, I saw leadership as something that came with titles and positions—a reward for hard work and competence. As I stepped into leadership roles, I realized that leadership is not about titles or accolades but rather responsibility. It's about being the one who makes the hard decisions, takes accountability when things go wrong, and lifts others up when they need support.

One of the biggest shifts in my understanding of leadership came when I realized that leadership is not about having all the answers. It's about being willing to ask the right questions, to admit when you don't know something, and to seek out the information or guidance you need. This realization had a profound impact on my relationships with those around me. I stopped feeling the need to present myself as the one who always had it all figured out. Instead, I embraced vulnerability. I became more open about the things I didn't know and in doing so, I created space for others to do the same. This shift in mindset allowed me to build deeper, more authentic relationships with my team, my colleagues, and the people I mentor. They no longer saw me as an untouchable figure at the top, but as someone who was still learning, still growing, still figuring it out—just like them.

This shift also made me a more empathetic leader. I started to see leadership not as a directive role but as a collaborative one. I began to value the input and perspectives of those around me more than ever before. I realized that leadership is not about being the smartest person in the room, but about surrounding yourself with smart people and creating an environment where their talents and insights can thrive. This new understanding of leadership not only deepened my relationships but also made me more effective in guiding others. It wasn't about showing them how to follow in my footsteps but helping them forge their own paths.

BREAKING FREE FROM COMPLACENCY: DEFINING MOMENTS OF GROWTH

There have been several pivotal moments in my life that prompted me to break free from complacency and reignite my hunger for growth. One such moment came during a conversation I had with a colleague who asked me, "What's next for you?" At the time, I didn't have an answer. I had achieved everything I had set out to do and for the first time in a long time, I realized I didn't have a plan. That question haunted me because it made me confront the uncomfortable truth that I had stopped dreaming. I had stopped pushing myself.

That moment of realization was both humbling and empowering. It reminded me that growth is a lifelong process and that no matter how much you've achieved, there is always more to learn, more to give, and more to become. That conversation reignited the fire within me and pushed me to seek out new challenges. I began to actively pursue opportunities that would push me out of my comfort zone, whether it was taking on new leadership roles, mentoring younger professionals, or speaking at events where I would have to be vulnerable and open about my journey.

Another defining moment came when I decided to remain connected to the community I came from, even though I had the financial means to live elsewhere. That decision wasn't just about proximity but rather staying rooted in the experiences that had shaped me. It was about remembering the hunger, the struggle, and the lessons that came from my younger years. By staying connected to that part of my life, I've been able to remain empathetic, grounded, and most importantly, hungry for more.

These moments have shaped my leadership style in ways I never anticipated. I now lead from a place of empathy and authenticity, understanding that leadership is not about having it all together but about being willing to grow, learn, and fail alongside those you lead. These experiences have also shaped the legacy I hope to leave. I want to be remembered not just as someone who achieved success but who helped others reach their potential. I want my legacy to be one of empowerment, where the people

I've led feel inspired to take risks, to grow, and to lead with integrity and empathy.

THE ONGOING JOURNEY OF LEADERSHIP AND GROWTH

The transition from complacency to leadership is not a one-time event but rather an ongoing process of growth, self-reflection, and intentionality. It requires confronting the internal and external challenges that keep us stuck in comfort and having the courage to step into the unknown. It's about evolving your understanding of leadership not as a position of power but as a responsibility to guide, support, and uplift those around you. And it's about breaking free from the limitations of the status quo, pushing yourself to grow even when it's uncomfortable and inspiring others to do the same.

At its core, leadership is about embracing the entire journey, the triumphs and the challenges and using those experiences to foster growth, both in yourself and in those you lead. It's about staying hungry, staying grounded in where you come from, and leading with authenticity, empathy, and a strong dedication to both personal and shared progress.

7

Cultivating Peace and Happiness: A Path to Inner Harmony

> *There is no way to happiness. Happiness is the way.*
> *There is no way to peace. Peace is the way.*
> Thich Nhat Hanh

TAKING CARE OF YOUR PEACE AND HAPPINESS IS LIKE maintaining your car. You wouldn't expect your car to run smoothly forever without an oil change or regular checkups. The same is true for your mental and emotional well-being. It's easy to think that once you've achieved a sense of peace or happiness, you're set. But peace, happiness, and fulfillment aren't static. They require regular maintenance, an active and ongoing process that ensures these qualities not only persist but also evolve as we do.

In my conversations with athletes, I often emphasize the distinction between merely wanting something and actively working for it. Many of us have desires, whether it's for happiness, success, or personal growth. Few take the next step to truly maintain those desires. It's in the maintenance where the real work happens. It's the difference between someone who dreams of running a marathon and someone who actually puts in the miles, week after week, to train.

When it comes to your inner-world, maintenance is more than just holding on to what you have. It's about cultivating the right conditions to thrive, which requires continuous effort and vigilance. Just as with physical fitness, maintaining mental and emotional well-being involves regular "workouts" by engaging in self-reflection, setting boundaries, and intentionally choosing your influences. The duality of maintenance lies in its ability to create opportunities and responsibilities simultaneously. When you achieve a new level of peace, happiness, or success, you have reached a starting point versus an endpoint.

The blessings we receive through financial gains, professional success, or personal contentment are not the final goal. They are opportunities that come with responsibilities. Just as you wouldn't buy a new house and let it fall into disrepair, you can't expect happiness or peace to remain without intentional upkeep. The responsibility may seem like a burden at times, but it's actually a privilege. The work you put in to maintain all you value keeps you thriving and opens doors to even greater growth.

INTERNAL VS. EXTERNAL: THE SOURCE OF TRUE HAPPINESS

One of the most common misconceptions about happiness is that it's tied to external factors. People often think that happiness is something they'll achieve once they hit a certain milestone, whether it's financial success, the perfect relationship, or career advancement. Here's the truth: Real, lasting happiness doesn't come from external sources. It comes from within. It's the result of regular internal maintenance and a commitment to fostering joy, peace, and fulfillment from the inside out.

This distinction between internal and external happiness is rooted in human psychology. Researchers have found that while external circumstances can bring temporary joy, they rarely create lasting fulfillment. This phenomenon is known as the "hedonic treadmill," where people quickly return to a baseline level of happiness after positive or negative events. In other words, external rewards such as money, possessions, or accolades don't create lasting happiness. Instead, it's the consistent internal work, the maintenance of our emotional and mental states that leads to sustained well-being.

When you actively engage in maintaining your happiness, you take responsibility for it. You no longer rely on external factors to dictate how you feel. You become more intentional about protecting your peace whether by avoiding toxic influences, confidently saying no when necessary, or creating healthy boundaries. This self-awareness and emotional intelligence allow you to remain steady, even when life throws challenges your way.

THE SACRIFICE BEHIND SUCCESS

When we talk about success, most people focus on the shiny, appealing aspects such as the accolades, recognition, and sense of accomplishment. What often gets overlooked is the sacrifice and stress that comes with creating that success. Whether you're working toward financial success, professional growth, or personal achievements, there's always a cost. The question becomes, are you willing to maintain your peace and happiness while pursuing success?

I've yet to meet a millionaire who got there without experiencing stress. The difference between those who are truly happy and those who are not isn't their bank account but rather their ability to maintain balance in other areas of their lives. The ones who are genuinely content are the ones who have figured out which stress is worth enduring and which areas of their lives need consistent care, such as their relationships, health, and personal time. They understand that their happiness isn't solely tied to their financial success. It's instead a byproduct of maintaining what brings them joy and fulfillment.

On the flip side, I've seen people who achieved great financial success but lost everything else along the way. Some went bankrupt, some fell into toxic relationships or lifestyles, and some even ended their lives because the stress became too much. It's a sobering reminder that success in any form is hollow without the maintenance of peace and happiness. The happiest people, whether they're millionaires or living on more modest means, are those who understand the value of maintaining their emotional and mental well-being.

Happiness isn't exclusive to wealth or material success. Some of the happiest people I know live with far fewer resources but have learned to prioritize what truly matters such as peace, family, and meaningful connections. They've mastered the art of maintaining their values, regardless of their financial situation. It's not about avoiding stress or hardship altogether, as that's impossible. It's instead about understanding what's worth investing your energy in and maintaining balance in the areas of your life that matter most.

THE POWER OF RECOGNIZING PERFECT DAYS

One of the most profound lessons in maintaining happiness is the importance of recognizing and appreciating perfect days, even if those days are made up of small moments. Too often, we get caught up in the negatives of the bad days, the challenges, and the frustrations to the point we fail to acknowledge the good. The more you practice noticing the positive experiences in your life, the more those moments begin to stand out. Over time, those positive moments accumulate, contributing to an overall sense of well-being and happiness.

This concept is supported by research in positive psychology, which shows that gratitude and mindfulness are powerful tools for increasing happiness. When you slow down and pay attention to the small joys in your life such as a beautiful sunset, a meaningful conversation, or a moment of peace, you train your brain to focus on the positive. This shift in awareness helps create a more pleasant life overall because you're no longer solely fixated on the negatives.

One practical way to do this is to count the perfect moments throughout your day. It doesn't have to be a grand event. It could be as simple as a peaceful cup of coffee in the morning or a smile from a stranger. These small moments add up and can reshape how you view your day and ultimately, your life.

AWARENESS AND THE VARIABLES OF HAPPINESS

Another key to maintaining happiness is increasing your awareness of the variables in your happiness equation. This means understanding what truly brings you joy and peace, and then actively cultivating those things. It also means recognizing what detracts from your well-being and learning how to limit the negative influences in your life.

Maintaining happiness is about more than just focusing on the good. It is equally essential to be mindful of the bad and understand how to navigate it. Slow down. Pay attention. Listen with your eyes and see with your ears. These practices can help you tune into the world around you and within you, allowing you to respond more thoughtfully to life's challenges and opportunities.

There's a lesser-known fact within human dynamics, namely the way we process external stimuli through our senses greatly impacts our emotional state. By being intentional about how you use your senses—listening deeply during conversations, observing body language, and noticing subtle shifts in energy—you can increase your emotional intelligence and become more attuned to what brings you peace and happiness.

YOUR BODY AS A TOOL FOR HAPPINESS

Finally, it's important to remember that your body is a tool for maintaining peace and happiness. Just as you maintain your mind and emotions, you must also maintain your physical well-being. There's a significant connection between physical health and emotional health. When you're tired, stressed, or run down physically, it becomes much harder to maintain mental and emotional balance.

Engaging in regular physical activity, eating nourishing foods, and getting enough sleep are all forms of maintenance that support your overall happiness. When your body feels good, it's easier to maintain a positive mindset and approach life's challenges with resilience.

THE COMMITMENT TO MAINTENANCE

Maintaining peace and happiness isn't a one-time event. It's an ongoing commitment to yourself and the things you value. It's about doing the regular maintenance whether through self-reflection, setting boundaries, practicing gratitude, or taking care of your physical health.

True happiness doesn't just happen but rather is cultivated. It's the result of being intentional about what you allow into your life, what you prioritize, and how you respond to challenges. When you take the time to do the maintenance work, you create the conditions for lasting peace and happiness, regardless of your external circumstances.

The next time you think about what makes you happy, ask yourself: What am I doing to maintain it? The answer will determine whether your peace and happiness are fleeting or enduring.

8

Trusting Your Instincts: Ancestral Wisdom for Modern Decisions

Trust your instinct. Intuition doesn't lie.
Oprah Winfrey

There's an old African proverb that says, **"The truth is like a Baobab tree: One person's arms cannot encompass it."** The wisdom behind this proverb reminds us that truth is vast, deep, and often beyond our immediate grasp. To understand it fully, we must trust our instincts and gather it piece by piece. Trusting yourself is no different. It is a journey of self-discovery that requires honesty, reflection, and faith in your own inner-compass. Yet in a world where external validation often takes precedence, trusting ourselves is a practice many of us have forgotten.

This lack of trust in oneself manifests in various ways. It's not that we don't have instincts or gut feelings. We do but too often, we dismiss them. We let our minds talk us out of what our hearts and bodies already know. Trusting yourself goes beyond simply acknowledging your challenges or strengths. It's about fully embracing your true life experiences, listening to the quiet voice within, and honoring it.

Think about the trust we place in others without question. When you step into an Uber, do you second-guess whether the driver knows the way? When you board a plane, do you question if the pilot is competent? Probably not. We trust these people to get us to our destination safely without a second thought. Yet we hesitate to trust ourselves in our own lives. We doubt our ability to steer our own course, even when our instincts scream for us to listen.

THE SILENT BETRAYAL OF SELF

I've seen people talk themselves out of their own instincts countless times. It's subtle but damaging. They dismiss the gut feeling that something's wrong or that a person's intentions are off. You've been there. You knew that person wasn't good for you, yet you gave them your number anyway against your better judgment. They got what they wanted and disappeared, leaving you wondering why you didn't trust yourself in the first place.

THE POWER OF SELF-REFLECTION AND INTUITION

Learning to trust yourself requires spending time with yourself. It means sitting quietly, tuning into your thoughts, and recognizing those intuitive moments. In today's fast-paced world, it's easy to ignore the voice inside, especially when there's so much noise coming from the outside from friends, family, social media, and societal expectations. The more you take time to reflect, the clearer your instincts will become.

For many young people, especially within the Black community, anxiety and gut feelings are often dismissed as mere nervousness. We learn to downplay those feelings because we're taught to be strong, to push through discomfort. That's where many mistakes happen. Someone pulls the proverbial trigger because they didn't trust their gut. Someone walks into a situation they knew wasn't right because they didn't take a moment to stop and listen. Trusting your truth and what you feel is real is a vital part of self-awareness and personal growth.

This doesn't mean you won't feel fear or doubt. In fact, those feelings are often a part of the process. Trusting yourself means having the courage to stand firm in your decisions, even when external pressure or doubt creeps in. It means making choices that are in your best interest, not because someone else thinks it's the right move but because you know it is.

THE WEIGHT OF DECEPTION

There's something to be said for trusting your instincts when it comes to deception, especially in situations where authority or power dynamics are at play. You don't always need validation for the feeling that someone is lying to you or manipulating you. You just know. That feeling in your gut is enough. When dealing with authority figures such as the police, for example, this instinct can be a matter of life and death.

I constantly remind my son to trust his gut, especially in situations where his safety is at stake. I tell him, "If something doesn't feel right, don't try to rationalize it away. Trust that feeling and act accordingly." Whether it's dealing with a police officer or navigating tricky social situations, trusting yourself is not about being self-righteous. It's about survival. The goal is to make it home safe and to make the best decisions possible in the moment. I've got his back, front, and middle, but he has to trust himself first.

Our human experience is deeply intertwined with our ability to sense, feel, and react to the world around us. Intuition has historically guided us through life's challenges, even when we couldn't fully explain why. It's the feeling beneath the surface, the sense of unease or certainty that helps us see beyond the facades people present. Trusting that part of yourself is crucial, not just in the obvious moments of danger or opportunity but in the day-to-day decisions that shape your life.

TRUSTING YOURSELF IN A DISTRACTING WORLD

In today's world, where we are constantly bombarded with information, opinions, and distractions, trusting yourself can feel like a revolutionary act. It requires tuning out the noise and tuning into your own voice. The more you practice it, the stronger that inner-voice becomes.

I tell my clients and my son the same thing: Don't let the world tell you who you are. Don't let society's expectations dictate your choices. Your gut knows more than you think. Honoring that wisdom within you is an act of self-respect and empowerment. It's easy to let others impose their will on you and to fall in line with what's expected. The more you trust yourself, the more you reclaim your power.

Honesty, self-reflection, and reclaiming your time are essential components of this process. When you trust your gut, you stop wasting time on people, situations, and opportunities that aren't right for you. You stop explaining yourself to people who don't deserve your time or energy. You begin to move with a sense of clarity and purpose because you know you're making decisions that are aligned with your truth.

EMBRACE THE TRUTH OF YOUR EXPERIENCE

Truth is vast and complex. It cannot be grasped all at once, and it certainly can't be contained by a single perspective. Trusting yourself is about embracing your own truth developed through your experiences, instincts, and gut feelings, then using that truth to guide your path.

When you trust yourself, you become more aware, more aligned, and more authentic. You make decisions that honor your growth and your well-being. You stop letting others define your choices or your worth. Most importantly, you begin to trust that you are capable of navigating whatever life throws your way not because you have all the answers, but because you trust yourself to find them.

Trust your gut. Trust your instincts. Most of all, trust that you already have within you the wisdom you need to live a life that is true to you.

9

Confronting the Past: Resolving Unfinished Business

Do or do not. There is no try.
Yoda from *Star Wars*

There's a quote from African American philosopher and activist W.E.B. Du Bois that speaks to the core of what it means to confront unfinished business in our lives. He said, "The chief problem in life is that of responsibility. How will you use your capabilities?" This question is not only about recognizing your potential but also about facing the moments when you've fallen short. Unfinished business, in its simplest form, is the lingering sense of missed opportunities, the dreams that never came to fruition, and the untapped potential we often leave unexplored. It's the moments when you know you could have given more but didn't. It's the goals you set but never pursued and the conversations you wish you'd had but were too afraid to start.

Unfinished business has a way of following you through life.

It's like a shadow that reminds you of what could have been. The college degree you never pursued, the career change you hesitated on, the project you abandoned halfway through are all remnants of unfinished business. The weight of these missed opportunities often stems from a lack of self-reflection, a reluctance to sit down with your experiences and fully understand them.

Without this crucial act of reflection, people find themselves repeating the same mistakes, trapped in cycles they don't even recognize. Patterns emerge, especially in relationships and decision-making. Have you ever noticed that some people date the same kind of partner over and over again, even though each relationship ends the same way? Or that they continually make poor financial decisions, leading to repeated bankruptcies? These patterns are symptoms of unfinished business. They are born out of an unwillingness to pause, reflect, and learn from life's lessons.

THE POWER OF SELF-REFLECTION

For many of us, the fear of confronting our unfinished business keeps us from reaching our full potential. Reflecting on my own journey, I realized that much of my hesitation and aversion to certain challenges came from judgments I internalized early on. I grew up in an environment where most of the kids weren't exposed to the opportunities I encountered. I remember being in spaces that felt foreign, where I was acutely aware of eyes on me making me feel judged, questioned, and as if I didn't belong. That feeling of being an outsider and of not fitting in stuck with me. It bred in me a determination to prove I did belong and to push beyond the limits others tried to impose on me.

That journey didn't start with action but rather reflection. It started with understanding the experiences that shaped me, the fears that held me back, and the potential that had yet to be realized. That is the true work of confronting unfinished business—acknowledging where you've fallen short or where you've let opportunities slip away and then committing to a path forward that honors your true potential.

UNFINISHED BUSINESS AND THE FEAR OF SUCCESS

Setting goals and recognizing your capacity to achieve them yet not taking the necessary steps to reach them is another form of unfinished business. Inaction is not just about avoiding failure. It's about consciously or unconsciously limiting yourself because you're not willing to make the necessary sacrifices. Many people operate in mediocrity not because they lack talent or ability but because they're afraid to step out of their comfort zone.

Unfinished business is about more than the results you see at the end of the journey. It's about the process—the willingness to invest in yourself, to push through discomfort, risk failure, and to grow. It's about recognizing that empowerment, nourishment, and enlightenment are byproducts of the journey itself, not the destination.

When I speak to young people, especially in our communities, I remind them of the tools they have at their disposal. Many of them carry around the answers to their biggest questions in the palm of their hand through their cell phones, their "handheld supercomputers." There is no excuse not to seek out the information you need, to invest in yourself intellectually and emotionally. But wanting something and actively working for it are two very different things. You can want change, but if you're not willing to leave that toxic relationship or step out of that dead-end job, you're still engaging with unfinished business. You're still stuck.

I've seen it so many times. Someone knows a relationship is bad for them, but they stay. He embarrasses her again, but she stays. He puts his hands on her and still, she stays. Each time you avoid confronting your unfinished business, you deepen the wound. True change requires not only recognizing the problem but taking action to move forward. It's about investing in real growth, not a superficial upgrade. Change doesn't come from hoping things will get better but rather from committing to bettering yourself.

THE TRAP OF SUPERFICIALITY

In our social media-driven world, it's easy to become caught up in shallow goals and superficial appearances. You see it all the time on Instagram, Facebook, or TikTok—the obsession with how things look rather than how they truly are. The rapper 50 Cent once said, "If your appearance is your largest asset, you are gonna do some hoe sh**." It's a blunt but necessary reminder that when you place too much value on appearances, you compromise your integrity and your potential.

Unfinished business often stems from this misalignment of values. When your goals are rooted in shallow pursuits such as physical appearance or material wealth, you're bound to feel empty once you reach them. Superficiality and depth don't coexist. To confront unfinished business, you must be willing to dig deeper and align your goals with what truly matters to you at your core. This is where introspection comes in. You have to ask yourself the hard questions: What do I really want? What am I willing to sacrifice to get there? What's holding me back?

By focusing on depth, on meaningful goals and values, you move away from the surface-level distractions and begin to align your actions with your true purpose. This process of reflection, alignment, and action is how you break free from the cycle of unfinished business.

THE RESPONSIBILITY OF ACTION

At the heart of unfinished business is a simple truth: Knowing what needs to be done is not enough. You must take action. When you delay action—whether out of fear, doubt, or complacency—you allow your unfinished business to build up like unpaid debt. Each missed opportunity, each untapped potential, adds weight to your spirit, making it harder to move forward.

The key to addressing unfinished business is aligning your goals with your core values and taking steps, however small, to achieve them. Whether it's leaving a toxic relationship, pursuing a long-abandoned dream, or investing in your personal growth, action is the antidote to regret. As Du Bois asks, "How will you use your capabilities?" The responsibility is yours.

True self-awareness requires acknowledging the unfinished business in your life and committing to a path of growth, reflection, and action. It requires a willingness to confront your fears, to push through discomfort, and to invest in your own empowerment. The process may be uncomfortable, but it's the only way to transform potential into purpose.

COMPLETING THE JOURNEY

Unfinished business is not just about what we failed to do. It's about the choices we continue to make. It's about the patterns we repeat because we haven't taken the time to sit with our experiences and learn from them. To complete the journey of self-awareness and personal growth, we must confront our unfinished business head-on. We must take action, not just in setting goals but in aligning our values, reflecting on our experiences, and committing to the hard work of personal transformation.

The African proverb mentioned earlier, "The truth is like a Baobab tree. One person's arms cannot encompass it," reminds us that growth is a collective journey—a process of gathering pieces of wisdom, learning from our past, and moving forward with intention. Unfinished business doesn't have to be a burden. It can be the catalyst for the next chapter of your life, a reminder that there is always room to grow, learn, and achieve the greatness that's already within you. The choice, as always, is yours.

10

Escaping the Trap of Familiarity

Familiarity breeds contempt.
Geoffrey Chaucer

There's an old saying, **"Voices fall dead on familiar ears."** It's a simple but powerful truth. When we hear advice or guidance repeatedly–especially from those closest to us such as parents, mentors, or even friends–it becomes easy to dismiss the message. It's not that the words aren't important, it's that familiarity has dulled impact. We become so accustomed to the messenger that the message itself is lost, buried beneath the layers of routine interaction and assumption.

We stop valuing the advice, not because it's wrong, but because we've grown too familiar with the voice delivering it. In the process, we sabotage our own growth by becoming deaf to wisdom that could be guiding us toward our dreams. The comfort of familiarity can lull us into a false sense of wisdom, making us think we know more than we do or that we've already heard everything worth hearing. It's precisely this trap of familiarity that keeps many people stuck, circling the same patterns and repeating the same mistakes.

FAMILIARITY BREEDS COMPLACENCY

When the voices around us become too familiar, we risk falling into complacency. It's easy to think we've internalized a message when in reality, we're merely hearing it without truly listening. This happens often in relationships with parents or long-term mentors who have been giving us advice our entire lives. After a while, their words start to sound like background noise. We stop listening because we think we already know what they're going to say. In doing so, we miss out on the deeper insights those familiar voices might still offer.

This complacency can be especially dangerous when it comes to our personal growth. Familiarity creates a sense of comfort, which can be good in moderation. It can also be a barrier to growth that requires discomfort. Growing demands that we stretch beyond what we already know and the voices we've grown used to hearing. To avoid this trap, we must actively seek out new perspectives, fresh voices, and individuals who will critique our thoughts.

THE VALUE OF EXTERNAL PERSPECTIVES

One of the most important lessons I've learned in my own journey is the value of involving external perspectives in my life and decisions. Familiarity tricks the brain into assuming we've conveyed or understood something fully when in reality, there are often gaps in our thinking that we can't see because we're too close to the situation. It's like trying to proofread your own writing. You miss the errors because you already know what you meant to say.

This is why it's essential to have someone outside of yourself who is removed from the situation to evaluate your thoughts, decisions, and actions. We all have blind spots. The only way to truly grow is to allow others to help us see what we can't. It's not about seeking validation or approval but rather inviting challenge and feedback. Growth happens when we're willing to listen to those who see the world differently than we do.

There's a reason why surrounding yourself with "yes men" is one of the quickest ways to stunt your personal and professional growth. It's easy to stay comfortable when everyone around you agrees with everything you say or do. That comfort is deceptive. It may feel like progress because you're not being challenged, but real change only comes when someone is brave enough to tell you the truth, even when it's uncomfortable. We don't need more people to nod along with us. We need people who push us to think bigger, dig deeper, and strive for greatness.

THE COMFORT OF DYSFUNCTION

Another dangerous aspect of familiarity is that it often breeds dysfunction. There's a strange but undeniable comfort in dysfunction, especially when it's all you've known. People stay in toxic relationships, make poor financial decisions, or engage in self-destructive behaviors not because they enjoy these things but because they're familiar. There's a certain predictability in dysfunction and humans are wired to seek out what's predictable, even if it's harmful.

The fear of change keeps many people locked in cycles of dysfunction. While change brings uncertainty, it also brings the possibility of something better. Breaking free from what's familiar, even when it's clearly detrimental, requires courage. It's not easy to walk away from a relationship, job, or habit that you've grown accustomed to, even when you know it's holding you back.

 Staying in the comfort of dysfunction comes at a cost. It keeps you from evolving, from reaching your full potential, and from experiencing true fulfillment. To grow, you must be willing to embrace the discomfort that comes with change. You must be willing to step into the unknown, to take risks, and to confront the possibility of failure. The comfort of knowing what comes next may feel safe, but it's also what keeps you from stepping into your greatness.

THE NECESSITY OF UNCERTAINTY

There's no real growth without risk. Success, awareness, and personal growth all require a level of uncertainty. The journey begins when you're willing to step into situations where you don't know what the outcome will be. It's easy to stay in a job you hate because it's predictable. It's easy to stay in a toxic relationship because you know what to expect. Real success and growth come from letting go of the need for certainty and embracing the unknown.

 Familiarity shackles you to the past. It keeps you stuck in patterns that no longer serve you. When you take the risk to step outside of your comfort zone, you open yourself up to new opportunities, new experiences, and new levels of awareness. You begin to see that the limitations you once believed were real are only illusions, created by your fear of change.

 Breaking free from the familiarity trap isn't just about making big changes in your life. It's about the small, everyday decisions that move you closer to your true potential. It's about saying no to the things that no longer serve you, even when they're comfortable. It's about choosing growth over complacency, even when it's hard. It's about surrounding yourself with people who challenge you rather than those who simply agree with everything you say.

BREAKING THE CYCLE OF FAMILIARITY

Personal growth requires us to break free from the cycles of familiarity that keep us stuck. Whether it's the voices we've grown too used to hearing, the dysfunction we've come to accept, or the comfort we find in predictability, familiarity is often the greatest barrier to our progress. To truly grow, we must actively seek out new perspectives, embrace discomfort, and be willing to confront the unknown.

The path to awareness and personal growth is not always smooth or predictable, but it is necessary. Surround yourself with people who push you to be better, who challenge your thinking, and who encourage you to step outside of what's comfortable. In doing so, you'll find that the greatest growth happens not in the safety of the familiar, but in the brave act of embracing the unknown.

Remember, the voices that challenge you are the ones that help you grow. The situations that feel uncomfortable are often the ones that push you toward your greatest potential. The unfamiliar path, though uncertain, is the one that leads to the most profound transformation.

Debriefing

Part II of *Be Still, Say Less* shifts the focus to cultivating stillness, emphasizing the power of connection, awareness, and intentionality in creating a fulfilling life. It delves into the practical aspects of building meaningful relationships, maintaining inner-peace, and trusting one's instincts. This section moves beyond individual self-awareness explored in Part I to how we interact with the world and others, highlighting the importance of being present and deliberate in those interactions.

KEY THEMES

- **Curating Connections:** Recognize the importance of surrounding oneself with positive influences that support personal growth. Curating connections emphasizes discerning authentic relationships and understanding how the company we keep shapes our direction in life.
- **Maintaining Peace:** Realize the necessity of making an ongoing effort to cultivate inner- peace and happiness.

This involves self-reflection, setting boundaries, practicing gratitude, and taking care of your physical well-being. It's about being intentional about what we allow into our lives and how we respond to challenges.

- **Trusting Your Instincts:** Honor your intuition and "gut feelings" as a source of wisdom. Learn the value of self-reflection to clarify instincts and the importance of trusting one's own truth, even when faced with external pressures or doubt. Know the importance of trusting instincts in situations involving deception or safety.
- **Confronting the Past:** Resolving "unfinished business" by reflecting on past experiences and committing to a path forward is essential. Confronting the past involves addressing the weight of missed opportunities and the importance of self-reflection to avoid repeating mistakes. It also touches on the fear of success and the need to align goals with true values.

Part II moves from introspection to interaction. It emphasizes that personal growth is not solely an individual journey but is deeply connected to our relationships and how we navigate the world. The section encourages readers to be active participants in shaping their environment and experiences rather than simply reacting to them. It highlights the importance of:

- **Intentional Relationships:** Choose to surround yourself with people who uplift and challenge you.
- **Mindful Living:** Be present and deliberate in daily actions and interactions.
- **Inner Guidance:** Trust your intuition and inner-wisdom.

- **Resolution and Growth:** Confront past issues and use them as opportunities for growth.

In essence, Part II is about building a life of purpose and fulfillment through conscious choices in relationships, self-care, and inner-guidance.

AFFIRMATION

I am committed to continuous learning and expanding my awareness in everyday moments.

SELF- REFLECTION

Part II focuses on how we interact with the world and others, moving beyond individual self-awareness to building meaningful connections, maintaining inner-peace, and trusting our instincts. Take some time to reflect on the following questions to deepen your understanding of the following themes.

1. Curating Connections:
- Who are the people I spend the most time with? Do these individuals uplift me, challenge me to grow, and support my values?
- Are there relationships in my life that drain my energy or leave me feeling negative? How can I set healthier boundaries in these relationships?
- Do I actively seek out connections with people who have different perspectives and experiences than my own?
- Am I discerning in who I let into my inner circle? How

do I decide who to trust and build deeper relationships with?

2. Maintaining Peace:
- What are my daily habits for maintaining inner-peace and happiness? Do I prioritize self-reflection, gratitude, and self-care?
- Am I mindful of the stories I tell myself? Are these stories empowering or limiting?
- What external factors or influences disrupt my peace? How can I minimize or manage these disruptions?
- Do I allow myself to feel and process emotions, including sadness, or do I tend to avoid them? How can I create space for emotional processing and healing?
- How do I balance pursuing success with maintaining my inner peace? What sacrifices am I making, and are they worth it?

3. Trusting Your Instincts:
- How well do I listen to and trust my gut feelings? Can I recall a time when I ignored my instincts and regretted it?
- Do I take time for quiet reflection to connect with my intuition? What practices help me tune into my inner wisdom?
- Am I able to stand firm in my decisions, even when faced with external pressure or doubt?
- In situations involving potential deception or safety, how effectively do I trust my instincts?
- Do I tend to second-guess myself or seek validation from others before making decisions?

4. Confronting the Past (Unfinished Business):
- What unfinished business am I carrying from my past? Are there missed opportunities or unresolved issues that weigh on me?
- Do I tend to repeat patterns in my relationships or decision-making? How can I break free from these cycles?
- Am I afraid of success? What sacrifices am I unwilling to make to achieve my goals?
- Do I invest in superficial goals or appearances, or am I aligned with my core values and true desires?
- What action steps can I take to address my unfinished business and move forward with intention?

5. Escaping the Trap of Familiarity:
- Are there voices or perspectives in my life that have become too familiar, causing me to dismiss their wisdom?
- Do I actively seek out external perspectives and challenge my own thinking?
- Am I comfortable with dysfunction simply because it's familiar? How can I break free from these patterns?
- Do I embrace uncertainty and change, or do I cling to predictability, even if it's limiting?
- What small changes can I make to step outside of my comfort zone and embrace new experiences?

By reflecting on these questions, you can gain deeper insights into how you connect with others, maintain your inner-peace, and navigate the world around you. This self-reflection will help you apply the principles of Part II to your own life and cultivate greater stillness and fulfillment.

Part III

Quiet Transformation: Unlocking Inner-Strength for Personal and Professional Growth

This section is about embodying the lessons learned and aligning our daily choices with our deeper values. It explores what it means to live with intention, to build discipline not from rigidity but from self-respect, and to pursue purpose with clarity and consistency. The focus is on integrating awareness into behavior—creating habits, setting boundaries, and showing up fully in our lives and communities. This is where the internal work begins to manifest outward, step by intentional step.

1

Redefining Success: Embracing Inner Growth

> *Success is liking yourself, liking what you do,*
> *and liking how you do it.*
> Maya Angelou

Fifth Avenue, New York City. I sat in a prime spot at a table surrounded by 10 highly driven and successful senior executives in a room where ambition buzzed in the air and everyone had already achieved more than most can imagine. One executive in particular caught my attention with his win-at-all-costs mentality. To him, winning was black and white—you either won the game or you lost. There was no middle ground, no room for interpretation.

That didn't sit right with me. I challenged his notion of success, explaining that winning isn't a standardized concept. What may look like success to one person could feel like failure to another. The real freedom, I told him, lies in **defining success for yourself.** When you create your own definition, you liberate yourself from the suffocating pressure of living up to other people's expectations.

For some, success is all about the bottom line—company stock prices, salaries, and climbing the corporate ladder. For others, it's about work-life balance, having time for family, or doing work that feels meaningful. I could see that my words made him uncomfortable. For someone who had spent his entire life chasing one definition of success, the idea that there could be multiple paths to "winning" was unsettling. Without self-awareness, without taking stock of your personal values, you can easily find yourself trapped in a definition of success that doesn't belong to you.

THE TRAP OF "GOLDEN HANDCUFFS"

This conversation reminded me of a harsh reality that millions of people live every day. They get up, go to work, and perform tasks they don't care about for companies they don't believe in. They chase the paycheck, the benefits, and the illusion of security. They are, as the saying goes, locked in "golden handcuffs." Sure, they might have a stable job and a comfortable salary but inside, they feel empty. Their work is not aligned with their values, and they're stuck in a cycle of dissatisfaction.

It's easy to say, "Well, why don't they just leave?" The truth is, those golden handcuffs can be hard to escape. The longer you stay in a situation that doesn't fulfill you, the harder it becomes to imagine life outside of it. Unfortunately for many people, the old saying is true: You can be bought.

I've seen this dynamic play out time and again. People stay in jobs because they're well-compensated but inside, they're miserable. As much as we don't want to admit it, it's tempting to stay in a situation that pays well, even when it's soul-crushing. This is where self-awareness becomes critical. You have to ask yourself, "Is my personal well-being worth the price I'm paying?"

EVALUATING ALIGNMENT: CORE VALUES VS. COMPANY PHILOSOPHY

When evaluating any job or opportunity, most people focus on two factors: The hours and the salary. That's it. Rarely do they take the time to reflect on the core values of the company and whether those values align with their own. Even fewer take inventory of the interpersonal dynamics of the workplace, including the culture and the people with whom they'll be spending the majority of their time. Both are just as important as the paycheck, if not more so.

Think about it: Do you really want to spend 40-plus hours a week with people you can't stand, people whose values are so misaligned with yours that it feels like a constant battle to maintain your integrity? I've worked in environments where I felt utterly isolated, even in a room full of people. It's a special kind of loneliness when you're surrounded by coworkers who don't understand or share your vision. Conversely, when you find a work environment that aligns with your values, the work becomes less about the paycheck and more about the purpose.

I've often asked people, "If you weren't getting paid, would you still do the work you're doing?" The answers are revealing. For many, the answer is a resounding "No." This doesn't mean you shouldn't care about making money, but it does highlight the importance of alignment between your values and the work you do.

THE DISCONNECT BETWEEN WEALTH AND HAPPINESS

Our society places a high value on material possessions and job titles. When you strip that all away, the real question becomes, "Are you happy?" When I meet new people, I don't care about what they do for a living. I'm more interested in how they feel about their life. Why? Because it's possible to have all the outward markers of success—money, cars, a nice house—and still be deeply unhappy.

We often equate wealth with happiness but time and again, research shows that there's no direct correlation between the two. I've met millionaires who were some of the unhappiest people I've ever encountered. Meanwhile, I've met people with far less in the way of material wealth who were living rich, fulfilling lives. Why? Because they had strong systems for maintaining peace, family, and communication—things that no amount of money can buy.

It's important to recognize that how you feel while working matters. We learned this during the COVID-19 pandemic when millions of people experienced burnout from jobs that didn't align with their values or well-being. Emotions impact sustainability, consistency, and discipline. If you hate every minute of your workday, it doesn't matter how much you're getting paid. Your situation is not sustainable in the long run.

TRUSTING YOURSELF AND DEFINING SUCCESS

Self-awareness is the foundation of personal and professional growth. As a therapist and executive leadership coach, I encourage everyone to start with a thorough self-evaluation. Take time to be still, to reflect on your feelings, and to assess whether you're living in alignment with your values. You are often the first to recognize when something is off, when healing is necessary, or when you need to make a change.

One of the most profound truths I've encountered is this: You are responsible for your own healing. No one else can do it for you. Healing is essential, not just in your personal life but in your professional world as well. Often the resentment or frustration we feel in our relationships or careers stems from unresolved issues within ourselves. When we don't feel worthy, we can't trust the love or respect others show us.

It's not enough to ask, "What do I do for a living?" Instead, ask yourself, "Am I happy? Does my work align with who I am and what I value?" These questions force us to look beyond the surface and evaluate whether we're living authentically or simply going through the motions to meet societal expectations.

BALANCING SELFLESSNESS AND SELF-CARE

In our society, selflessness is often held up as a virtue. We're told that putting others first is a sign of strength and character. But when you consistently put others ahead of yourself, you risk devaluing your own well-being. This can lead to burnout, exploitation, and a diminishing sense of self-worth. The ability to set boundaries, say "No," and prioritize yourself is not selfish but rather essential for your mental and emotional health.

I often tell people, "You cannot pour from an empty cup." If you're constantly giving to others without replenishing yourself, you'll eventually run dry. Prioritizing yourself is not about disregarding others. It's about recognizing that you are your greatest asset. If you take care of yourself first, you'll be in a much better position to care for others.

REDEFINING INFLUENCE IN THE AGE OF SOCIAL MEDIA

In today's world, attention has become the ultimate currency. Social media influencers have millions of followers but the question is, "What are they influencing?" During a conversation with a young woman who identified herself as an influencer, I asked, "What do you influence?" Her response? "I have 1.3 million followers." When pressed further, it became clear that the number of followers was the focus, not the substance of what she was influencing.

This is the problem with chasing attention rather than meaningful impact. True influence should be about more than just numbers. It should be about making a positive, lasting change in the world. When your focus shifts from appearance to authentic impact, you redefine what it means to be successful.

CRAFTING YOUR OWN PATH

At the end of the day, your life is yours to design. Whether in your career, your relationships, or your personal growth, it's up to you to define what success looks like. The key is to trust yourself, listen to your intuition, and align your actions with your values. True success isn't about meeting someone else's standards. It's about living authentically on your own terms.

As you continue on this journey of self-awareness and personal growth, remember to check in with yourself regularly. Ask the hard questions. Are you happy? Are you fulfilled? Are you living in alignment with your values? If the answer is "No," have the courage to make a change.

2

Returning to the Authentic Self: A Journey Within

> *When you reach the end of what you should know, you will be at the beginning of what you should sense.*
> Khalil Gibran

THE BODY IS A PERFECT HARD DRIVE, STORING TERABYTES of information from our lived experiences. Every touch, breath, sorrow, and joy is logged deep within us, waiting to be uncovered. As I began my own journey toward self-awareness, I realized that emotions are not just fleeting responses. They are the body's way of communicating, of speaking a truth that my mind sometimes refuses to hear. Thoughts may shape the vocabulary of the mind, but emotions form the language of the body. When the two unite, real magic happens.

For years, I'd operated primarily from my head. I relied on logic and reasoning, trusting my brain to get me through complex decisions. The wisdom in my head was strategic, calculated, always weighing pros and cons. Yet in moments of profound truth, something else would surface—an inexplicable sensation that came not from rational thought but from somewhere deeper. It was a twinge in my gut, a tightening in my chest, a sudden sense of unease or peace. This wasn't cognitive wisdom but instead the body's intuition speaking.

As I sat with these feelings, I came to understand that true balance and harmony require the union of these two wisdoms. The head and the body, logic and intuition, must work together. It is not enough for something to make sense in your mind. It must also feel right in your body. This is a crucial step in uncovering your core self.

Often we undervalue bodily knowledge. We dismiss gut feelings and the tension in our muscles, opting instead for what logically "should" be right. In doing so, we ignore half of the wisdom available to us. Our ancestors, though many lacked formal education, understood this balance. They did not have access to modern psychological theories or cognitive science. They knew instinctively to trust their bodies.

I think about my grandmother often when I reflect on this. Her wisdom wasn't from books but from life. She knew when a storm was coming because she could feel it in her bones. She dreamed of fish when someone in the family was pregnant. It may sound like folklore, but it was a form of deep, embodied knowledge, of wisdom passed down through generations of lived experience. When my hand itched, she'd say, "You're coming into some money." I'd laugh but somewhere in me, I believed her. That's the kind of trust in the body that modern life often strips away from us.

James Baldwin once wrote, "You think your pain and your heartbreak are unprecedented in the history of the world, but then you read." His words from *The Price of the Ticket* resonate deeply because they remind me that our struggles are part of a broader human experience. Just as our bodies hold the wisdom of our personal experiences, they also carry the collective knowledge of those who came before us. To trust ourselves is to trust this lineage of wisdom. It's to recognize that our core selves are not only shaped by our individual experiences but are part of a much larger narrative.

Our ancestors were summa cum laude in the school of life, as I like to say. They faced the unimaginable and still managed to thrive. How? They honored both the knowledge of the mind and the wisdom of the body. This dual intelligence is something we must reclaim. When I began listening to the signals from my body—the racing heart before a wrong decision, the weight in my shoulders after a hard conversation—I started making better choices, not just logically sound ones. I made choices that felt right in the deepest parts of me.

This requires stillness. In our fast-paced world, there's little room for reflection. We're encouraged to rush forward, decide quickly, and keep moving. But the body doesn't work on those terms. It speaks in whispers, in subtle cues that are easy to miss if we're not paying attention. Self-awareness, the uncovering of the core self, begins with learning to pause and listen to these whispers. Like the "check engine" light in a car, our bodies give us warning signs. They tell us when something isn't right, when we need to slow down, when we need to dig deeper.

Learning to trust myself meant learning to trust those bodily signals, even when they contradicted the seemingly logical path. It was subtle at first. A tingle of discomfort when a situation wasn't as harmless as it seemed. A warm sense of relief when I made the right decision, even when it didn't make sense on paper.

Success, I've learned, is in the details. The body knows details that the mind often overlooks. While your mind may focus on the present moment and what's visible, your body's intuition is attuned to what lies beneath the surface. It sees what's coming, even if you don't yet. When you honor this, when you allow your cognitive wisdom and your body's intuition to work in harmony, you are finally aligned with your core self.

In our journey toward self-awareness, we must embrace this integration. We must honor both the logic of the mind and the intuition of the body, trusting that both are necessary for a life lived in balance and authenticity. In doing so, we reconnect not only with ourselves but with the wisdom of those who came before us.

3

Navigating the Spaces that Shape Us

What separates privilege from entitlement is gratitude.
Brené Brown

GROWING UP, I FOUND MYSELF IN SPACES THAT FELT galaxies away from my public housing beginnings. Elementary school introduced me to a world where two-parent households were the norm with parents who were doctors, lawyers, and accountants. My mother, through sheer determination and countless sacrifices, found a way to make sure I was there in that school, despite the financial gap between us and those families. While people smiled politely, there was an underlying current of judgment, a palpable sense that I might not fully belong. The hierarchy was clear: I could be there, but I didn't have the same status as the other kids. My mom, despite her strength, wasn't like the minivan-driving soccer moms who dominated PTA meetings.

As a child, I couldn't quite articulate what I was feeling, but

I knew something was different. The innocence of childhood allowed me to recognize the dissonance, even if I couldn't name it. "You're mean!" a six-year-old might declare when faced with discomfort. Simple, direct, and unapologetic. But as I grew older, I learned to rationalize those feelings, projecting layers of cognition onto them until they became tangled with self-doubt.

It wasn't until years later that I truly appreciated the depth of what my mother had done for me. She managed to get me into an elite school and send me on a trip to Australia on a salary of $35,000 a year. That in itself was a triumph. As Maya Angelou wrote, *And Still I Rise*. Despite the financial disparity, despite not driving the Lexus or the Benz, my mother rose. In doing so, she gave me the same right to occupy those spaces.

Once we got past the initial maze of elitism, a new layer of hierarchy emerged. It wasn't just about being there but rather became about who was paying full tuition and who was receiving assistance. While I never fully fit into either group, I began to see the complexity of the system. I wasn't just navigating a space that was unfamiliar. I was experiencing the weight of what it meant to exist in that space while carrying my mother's sacrifices with me.

When the time came to decide where I would go for high school, I was awarded a scholarship to a private school. I was overjoyed at the prospect of continuing my education in familiar surroundings, building on the connections I'd made. My mom, ever the visionary, said, "You've spent enough time in this bubble." At the time, I was devastated. How could she make that decision for me after I had worked so hard to earn the scholarship? Looking back, I see her wisdom.

Brené Brown captures this kind of understanding perfectly in her book *Daring Greatly* when she says, "You either walk inside your story and own it or you stand outside your story and hustle for your worthiness." My mom knew that I had more to learn outside the bubble, that real-world experience would give me the strength to not just survive but thrive. She wanted me to own my story, to live fully in the reality of my background without feeling as if I had to hustle to belong.

Public school, as it turned out, became one of the best decisions she made for me. I learned how to navigate diverse environments, connect with people from all walks of life, and draw strength from the stories of those around me. Now when I step into Fortune 500 boardrooms, I feel as comfortable as I do in the backroom, that sacred space in the Black community where wisdom was shared and connections were made.

In those backrooms, I met people such as Stick Man. His struggles were real and included a battle with crack addiction that defined much of his life, but his insights were profound. "There really ain't such a thing as extra money," he'd say. "It's all just money." His perspective was one of survival but beneath the surface, it was about more than that. Stick Man understood something about life that took me years to fully grasp: Resources, whether financial, emotional, or spiritual, are tools. It's not about how much you have but how you use what's in front of you.

Stick Man had mastered the art of seeing opportunity where others saw none. He found ways to get by every day, despite waking up with no money and no prospects. It made me think: "What if we all had that ability? What if we could see opportunity everywhere, not just in a survival sense but in a way that allowed us to thrive?" Stick Man's approach was dysfunctional, yes, but the mindset was one of resilience. Resilience, as Brown tells us, is a skill that comes from embracing vulnerability, not shying away from it.

So often, we judge people such as Stick Man. We dismiss their wisdom because of their circumstances. The truth is, everyone has something to teach us. Stick Man taught me that real self-awareness comes from understanding that we are not separate from our experiences but rather shaped by them.

When I reflect on my journey — from those affluent elementary school classrooms to the backrooms where Stick Man shared his stories — I see that my core self is a combination of both worlds. I've learned to own my story, to walk fully in it, and to recognize the power in the lessons life has handed me. As Brown says in her book *Daring Greatly: How the Courage to Be Vulnerable Transforms the Way We Live, Love, Parent, and Lead*, "Vulnerability is not winning or losing. It's having the courage to show up and be seen when we have no control over the outcome." That's what Stick Man did every day, and that's what my mom did for me by making wise choices on my behalf.

The spaces we navigate in life are not always easy, but they are always ours. By embracing the totality of our experiences, by showing up in both the boardroom and the backroom, we uncover the core of who we are.

4

Awakening Inner-Strength through Gratitude and Appreciation

Gratitude turns what we have into enough.
Anonymous

GRATITUDE, I'VE LEARNED, IS MORE THAN JUST A POLITE "Thank you" or a gesture of courtesy. It's a way of seeing, a way of being. To live with gratitude is to live with a heightened awareness of the world around you, to recognize the intricate web of support, kindness, and connection that carries you through each day. The journey toward deepening my awareness began when I realized just how much I had been taking for granted.

There was a time when I moved through life largely unaware of the small yet significant moments that deserved recognition. I focused on what needed fixing, what hadn't gone right, or what felt incomplete. I wasn't fully seeing the richness that was all around me. It wasn't that I didn't appreciate the people in my life or the opportunities I had. It was that I wasn't consciously making space for gratitude. Consequently, my awareness of myself and the world felt diminished, as though I was only moving through the motions.

The turning point came during a particularly stressful season in my life. I was overwhelmed by work and personal challenges, feeling disconnected from myself and those around me. It was during this time that a close friend began dropping off meals for me without asking, just quietly leaving them at my doorstep. I appreciated it, of course, but I didn't fully grasp the depth of what she was offering me. It wasn't until weeks later, when I sat down to write her a thank-you note, that I realized the magnitude of her kindness.

Writing that note opened my eyes to the power of acknowledgment. I became more aware of how supported I had been, not just by her but by many others in my life. That simple act of writing, of saying, "I see what you did for me, and I'm grateful," helped me tap into a deeper understanding of connection. It made me realize that gratitude, at its core, is about seeing. It's about opening your eyes wide enough to notice the gifts life is offering you, even when those gifts come wrapped in difficulty or challenge.

As I began to practice this awareness, I noticed how much I had been missing. I noticed the small moments that were filled with love, such as my partner making me coffee in the morning or the way a colleague stayed late to help with a project. These moments had always been there, but I hadn't truly been present for them. Gratitude made me present. It brought me into the now, into the fullness of each experience.

In both personal and professional settings, gratitude plays a vital role in shaping how we experience the world. At work, I started paying closer attention to the efforts of my colleagues. I made it a point to express appreciation, not just for the major successes but for the small, everyday acts of diligence and kindness. I saw how this shifted the dynamics in the office. Morale improved, yes, but more importantly, people began to feel seen. Gratitude, I discovered, creates a bridge of connection, one that allows people to feel valued and acknowledged.

This same awareness of gratitude has profoundly shaped my personal relationships. I've learned that expressing appreciation, especially for the small things, deepens bonds. In a world where so much goes unnoticed, taking the time to acknowledge the little gestures, the small acts of kindness, opens up a space for empathy and compassion. It fosters a sense of reciprocity, a flow of giving and receiving that nurtures relationships on a deeper level. It isn't just about the act of saying "Thank you." It's about recognizing the humanity in the other person, the shared experience of being in this life together.

Gratitude, I've come to understand, is an essential part of human beingness. It's what connects us to each other and to ourselves. When we practice gratitude, we tune into the abundance that already exists in our lives. We stop focusing on what's lacking or what hasn't gone our way, and we begin to see the fullness of what is. In that shift, we become more resilient, more open, and more present to the richness of the human experience.

There's a shift that happens when you begin to cultivate gratitude as a daily practice. You start to see the world differently. It's as if your awareness becomes sharper and your senses more attuned to the good that surrounds you. This isn't just a matter of being optimistic or positive. It's about living in a way that is grounded in the reality that life, even with its struggles, offers countless moments of grace.

When I reflect on my journey toward awareness, I see how gratitude has served as a powerful guide. It has taught me to pause, reflect, and honor both the large and small ways that life supports me. Gratitude has brought me closer to myself, allowing me to see not only what others have done for me but also what I've done for myself. It has reminded me to thank myself for my own resilience, for the ways I've shown up in my life, even when it was hard.

To be grateful is to acknowledge the interconnectedness of all things. It's to recognize that we are never truly alone, that our lives are woven together with the lives of others in ways both seen and unseen. This awareness transforms how we move through the world. It allows us to navigate life's challenges with more grace, to face adversity with a mindset of abundance rather than scarcity.

Gratitude at its heart is a practice of heightened awareness. It calls us to recognize the beauty and support already woven into our lives, to find richness in both the everyday and the extraordinary. By embracing gratitude, we not only lift up those around us but also deepen our own sense of presence grounded in connection, compassion, and a growing recognition of the gifts life continually offers.

5

Unlocking Potential Through Trust and Guidance

> *A mentor holds up a mirror, revealing the parts of*
> *ourselves we often overlook.*
> Dr. Thurman E. Webb, Jr.

MENTORSHIP IS ONE OF THE MOST VALUABLE TOOLS FOR self-awareness and personal growth, regardless of where you are in life. Whether you're just starting out, navigating through a mid-point, or finding your way at a more advanced stage, the right mentor can be transformative. A mentor offers wisdom, guidance, and most importantly, perspectives that are often difficult to access on your own. Having someone who's been down a similar path helps you not only avoid common pitfalls but also make more informed decisions along the way.

In my own journey, mentorship has been pivotal. I've been both a mentee and a mentor, and these relationships have enriched my personal and professional life in ways I hadn't anticipated. I think back to one of my earliest mentors who gave me a truth I wasn't ready to hear at the time. "Your problem," he told me, "is that you think you're above average, but you're really just average because you hang around people who are below average." Initially, his words stung. How could I be average? I was putting in the work and felt that I was achieving more than those around me. That was exactly his point: I was measuring myself against the wrong standard.

I realized he wasn't diminishing my potential. He was pushing me to expand beyond my current environment. That moment of uncomfortable truth was a wake-up call, one that forced me to reflect on the company I kept, the conversations I was having, and the actions I was taking. It was through this lens that I began to see the real power of mentorship. A mentor holds up a mirror, showing you parts of yourself that you either can't see or refuse to acknowledge. Without this mirror, it's easy to remain stagnant, believing you're making progress when in fact, you're stuck.

That experience taught me one of the most fundamental aspects of mentorship: Trust. You have to trust your mentor to give you the truth, even when it's uncomfortable. Without that trust, the relationship loses its value. If I hadn't trusted my mentor at that moment, I could have easily dismissed his feedback, chalked it up to his misreading of my situation, and continued down the same path. Because I trusted him, I listened. I sat with the discomfort, evaluated my choices, and ultimately made changes that propelled me forward. Trust is everything in a mentor-mentee relationship. The deeper the trust, the more willing you are to take your mentor's advice seriously, even when it's hard to hear.

Mentorship, however, is not just about receiving advice. It's also about gaining perspective. A mentor can help you see the bigger picture, offering clarity when the future seems uncertain or the path ahead feels unclear. I've seen this both as a mentee and a mentor. When my mentees come to me with questions about their careers or personal challenges, I don't just offer solutions. Instead, I help them see how their immediate goals fit into the larger context of their lives. It's about zooming out, taking a step back, and looking at the broader landscape. Sometimes the guidance a mentee needs is less about the specific problem at hand and more about aligning their goals with a long-term vision.

One of the things I cherish most about mentoring is watching my mentees grow, surpassing even the heights I've reached. It's not about me but them achieving their potential faster and more efficiently than I did. That's the beauty of a good mentor-mentee relationship. A mentor should want their mentee to succeed, to soar beyond the limits they themselves faced. Look at relationships such as Oprah Winfrey and Maya Angelou, or Warren Buffett and Bill Gates. The mentees surpassed their mentors financially, but that's not the point. The point is that a good mentor doesn't need to hold the spotlight. Their greatest success is in seeing you win.

Over the years, I've had several mentors. Each has offered a different perspective, a different kind of expertise. Now I find myself in the role of mentor to others. Some of my mentees have become like family to me. Three of them, in fact, are now my godchildren. We even take vacations together every year. One is a clinical psychologist in the Air Force, another is a sports psychologist at the University of Notre Dame, and the youngest just earned her master's in counseling psychology and is preparing for her Ph.D.

It's fulfilling work. When I mentor them, I approach it with the mindset of, "How much quicker could I have gotten here if I had a 'me' guiding me?" I listen carefully to their challenges and help them navigate not just their professional goals, but the external factors that inevitably impact those goals. Once they see the value of our relationship, I open up my entire playbook of resources, teaching them not only how to access these tools but also how to manage the responsibility that comes with them.

One thing that remains true in all mentorship relationships is that the mentor's advice is unbiased. Because the mentor has no personal stake in the mentee's decisions, they can offer feedback rooted purely in the mentee's best interest. This objectivity is crucial. Without it, it's hard to get a clear perspective on your actions and decisions. As a mentor, my only goal is to see my mentees succeed in a way that aligns with their values and long-term aspirations. That clarity of purpose helps cut through the noise and provides the mentee with a sense of reassurance when making tough decisions.

Another unexpected but invaluable benefit of mentorship is the opportunity for networking. One of my roles as a mentor is to introduce my mentees to people they wouldn't otherwise have access to, leveraging my own relationships to open doors for them. Networking through mentorship expands one's community, creating opportunities for personal and professional growth. It's not just about who you know but rather fostering meaningful relationships with people who can provide support and guidance in your journey.

Mentorship is a relationship built on trust, truth, and mutual growth. It's not a one-way street. As much as I've helped my mentees grow, they've helped me grow as well. They keep me sharp, asking questions and approaching problems in ways that challenge me to think differently. That's the beauty of the mentor-mentee dynamic. It's a partnership where both parties evolve together.

Mentorship is about recognizing the untapped potential in

someone, helping them bring it to life, and finding joy as they exceed even your own accomplishments. It creates a ripple effect, where those who were once guided step into the role of mentor themselves, sharing the lessons they've learned. Looking back at the mentors who shaped my journey, I realize their most valuable gift wasn't just the knowledge they imparted. It was their belief in my ability to grow and the guidance they offered to help me reach that next horizon.

6

Harnessing the Power of Connection

*It's not just who you know, but who knows you and
values your presence in their world.*
Dr. Thurman E. Webb, Jr.

Networking is more than just a business strategy. It's an essential part of self-awareness and personal growth. In today's interconnected world, the relationships we build often determine the opportunities we encounter and the lessons we learn. But what does networking truly mean, and why is it so important? The traditional saying, "It's not what you know, but who you know," has been revised in my mind to, "It's not just who you know, but who knows you." To grow and succeed, particularly in the business world, making your presence felt authentically is crucial.

The importance of networking cannot be underestimated, especially in today's multifaceted professional landscape. Networking opens doors to opportunities for employment, advancement, and personal connections. It's not just about shaking hands or exchanging business cards. Real networking is about building genuine relationships with people who see your value, who know you and can vouch for you when the right opportunity arises.

Let me tell you about one of the most pivotal moments in my career that underscores the power of networking. A good friend called me one day and told me about a think tank pilot program. Someone had dropped out, and she thought I would be a perfect fit. This wasn't a paid opportunity, and I didn't know much about the people involved but I trusted her judgment. Within my circle, we honor each other's recommendations. I accepted the offer, even though it wasn't exactly what I was looking for at the time.

The think tank included Hollywood producers, CEOs, prominent mental health professionals, and bestselling authors. By stepping into this space, I gained exposure and built relationships that I could never have predicted. Many of those connections turned into collaborative opportunities. The leader of the think tank appreciated my unique approach and from there, I started networking with CEOs worldwide. Opportunities that would have taken me years to access on my own were suddenly within reach.

This experience taught me a critical lesson: Networking is about staying ready so you don't have to get ready. It's about being open to new opportunities, even if they don't come packaged the way you expect. It's about entering spaces with confidence and humility, bringing your authentic self to the table. The moment you stop being yourself, you lose the special ingredient that makes you valuable. In that think tank, I didn't pretend to be anyone other than who I was, and that authenticity opened doors I hadn't even known existed.

Networking is not just about the immediate payoff but rather planting seeds that may grow into opportunities down the line. Today, someone may be a business partner. Tomorrow, they might be a key contact or friend. In many ways, networking is a time-sensitive endeavor. You have to be proactive, constantly expanding your web of contacts. This isn't about being opportunistic or calculating. It's about genuinely connecting with people, being a good listener, and bringing something of value to the relationship.

One of the most practical benefits of networking is that it can help you find jobs, connect with others who share your interests, and build lasting relationships. The key to effective networking, however, isn't to walk into the conversation asking for something. It's to create a space for mutual benefit. The goal is not to ask for jobs or favors outright. That can happen, but it shouldn't be the driving force. Instead, it's about building relationships based on shared interests and goals.

Start by assessing the network you already have. You likely know more people than you think from school, work, hobbies, and family. Take a look at your social media accounts. Who follows your updates? Who engages with your content? These are all part of your network. With today's technology, you don't have to rely on letters or long-distance calls to stay in touch. A quick message, text, or direct message can serve as an initial point of contact, allowing the other person to guide the conversation in a way that works for them.

Networking, like any skill, takes practice. One important element is timing. Not every contact wants a call in the middle of their workday, and not every person will be available when it's convenient for you. Respecting their time and preferences is crucial. I often prefer to make initial contact through a text or DM, allowing the person to set a time that works for them. Once that conversation happens, I always express genuine gratitude for their time and, if appropriate, ask if they know anyone else who might be able to share additional information.

Another key networking strategy is joining professional associations. These organizations offer opportunities to meet people who share your career concerns and aspirations. By attending association meetings, you not only learn more about your field but also build a network of people who can support your career journey. This networking is not just about making professional connections. It's about deepening your understanding of your industry and expanding your sense of what's possible.

I once met someone at a networking event who was struggling to find a job. I suggested they join LinkedIn, as their industry was well-represented there. After beefing up their profile and writing a few thoughtful articles, they landed an informational interview that eventually turned into a job offer. The key wasn't just that they were on LinkedIn. It was that they used the platform to showcase their expertise and connect with others in a meaningful way.

Social media has made networking more accessible than ever. Platforms such as LinkedIn, X, Instagram, and even blogs allow you to share your thoughts, skills, and experiences with a global audience. While face-to-face connections remain powerful, online networking opens doors to people you might never meet in person. Remember, though, that networking is still about human connection. Whether online or offline, people remember how you make them feel. A warm, genuine interaction is far more impactful than a polished elevator pitch.

Networking is also about reciprocity. Just as you seek to benefit from others, you should look for ways to offer support and resources to those in your network. It's incredibly gratifying when you can help someone else succeed, whether by offering advice, sharing a resource, or introducing them to someone who can help them achieve their goals. Networking is a partnership and the more you give, the more you'll get back in return.

The truth is, many of the best opportunities come through connections. Did you know that the majority of employees at most organizations were hired through someone they knew? Letting people in your network know that you're seeking opportunities can be one of the most effective strategies for finding a new job or growing your career. You don't have to know someone well to ask for advice or guidance. Sometimes, it's the person you barely know who provides the key connection to your next big opportunity.

Networking isn't just about advancing your own goals. It's about creating a community of people who help one another succeed. Even relationships that might not seem immediately beneficial can turn into something valuable over time. Helping to connect two people in your network who don't know each other, for instance, can have a ripple effect that benefits both of them and ultimately you as well.

When done right, networking is one of the most powerful tools for personal growth. It expands your awareness of the world, opens your eyes to new possibilities, and reinforces the idea that we are all connected in some way. It's about more than just advancing your career. It's about building meaningful relationships that support both personal and professional growth. Stepping outside of our own bubbles to embrace this interconnectedness can bring about immense happiness, not only for ourselves but for those we connect with along the way.

7

Branding and Networking: Catalysts for Progress

A strong brand opens doors, but authentic connections create lasting opportunities.
Dr. Thurman E. Webb, Jr.

BRANDING AND NETWORKING ARE OFTEN SEEN AS separate, but they are like fraternal twins sharing the same DNA yet distinct in their impact. Understanding the distinction between them is critical for anyone looking to accelerate their career or personal development. Together, successful branding and networking can propel you forward, helping you stand out from the crowd and create opportunities. While personal branding is about what we want others to see and believe about us, networking is about how others actually perceive us. There's a nuanced interplay between the two, and it's this combination that ultimately drives success.

Branding is about crafting an image of yourself that represents who you want to be and how you want to be perceived. It's why we dress for the job we want before we've even gotten it. Just as the Nike swoosh or McDonald's golden arches immediately evoke their brands, our personal brand is what we project to the world. It's the skills, expertise, and body of work we can showcase at any given moment. The better our brand, the easier it is to pitch ourselves to clients, employers, and audiences.

Networking is where the rubber meets the road. It's not enough to craft the perfect personal brand. Networking is where people see the real you and form perceptions based on their interactions with you. You can have an impeccable personal brand but if you're not building relationships and connecting with people meaningfully, that brand will only take you so far. The power lies in blending both to shape how you're seen through branding and reinforce that image by how you show up and build relationships through networking.

In 2014, after the deaths of Trayvon Martin and Tamir Rice, I found myself confronting the harsh reality of how Black men were being branded in America. Trayvon's tragic death was painful enough but it was the death of Tamir, a 12-year-old boy shot by police while playing in a park, that pushed me to action. It became clear that mainstream society had imposed a negative, harmful brand on Black men, one rooted in fear, suspicion, and violence. I couldn't find a space showcasing the contributions of Black men working to make the world a better place, so I decided to create one.

That's how *Rebrand the Black Man* was born. What started as an Instagram movement quickly grew into a full-fledged nonprofit within a year and a half. The mission was simple: Highlight the contributions of Black men and create a new narrative around our identity. Whether we liked it or not, society was branding us every day. It was time for us to take control of that narrative.

Rebranding is about reshaping perception. It's about telling the story we want told and projecting the image that reflects who we truly are. But branding alone wasn't enough to counter the negative perception surrounding Black men. Networking became equally important. As I began meeting Black men who embodied this new brand—men who were community leaders, business owners, educators, and more—I started to build a network. Many of these men didn't realize how much they were already contributing to rebranding Black men. They were living proof that the mainstream narrative didn't hold up, but they hadn't been recognized for the ways they changed the narrative.

I approached these men, often at random, to express my gratitude for their representation. Some were confused at first but once I explained the mission, they got it. We started building a network that included Black men from all walks of life—millionaires, factory workers, lawyers, teachers, and more. If you were contributing positively to your community, you were part of the rebrand.

As the network grew, so did our impact. We facilitated conversations between established professionals and younger men seeking mentorship. It became clear that branding wasn't just about changing how the world saw us. It was also about connecting and lifting each other up. Networking became the bridge that turned branding into action. It allowed us to leverage our connections to create new opportunities, not just for ourselves but for the next generation.

Networking, at its core, is about building meaningful relationships. It's about expanding your reach by connecting with people who share your values and vision. Every conversation and introduction is an opportunity to grow and learn. It's not about advancing your own interests alone but rather finding ways to support others and help them succeed as well.

I've seen firsthand how the power of a network can propel you to new heights. When I joined a think tank of influential leaders, I didn't know where it would lead. There was no paycheck, and I wasn't even sure what I was stepping into. The relationships I built led to collaborations and opportunities I couldn't have imagined. Some of the people I met in that think tank connected me to CEOs and thought leaders around the world, expanding my network further.

The key lesson here is that networking is not transactional. It's not about asking for favors or expecting immediate returns. It's about building relationships based on mutual respect and shared values. The more genuine your connections, the more impactful your network becomes.

Branding and networking may operate in different worlds, but when they come together, they create a powerful synergy. Your brand attracts people to you, while your network allows you to sustain and build on those relationships. Together, they create a pathway to career advancement, personal growth, and ultimately, a legacy.

As *Rebrand the Black Man* continues to grow, I'm reminded daily of the importance of these twin forces. Branding allows us to reshape narratives, while networking helps us create lasting change. Whether in your personal or professional life, these twin engines can help you craft a future that reflects who you truly are. So be intentional with your brand, build genuine connections, and watch the opportunities unfold.

8

Fueling Personal Growth through Creative Transformation

Creativity disrupts the ordinary, shifting us beyond routine and unlocking new doors to growth and deeper possibilities.
Dr. Thurman E. Webb, Jr.

WHEN WE THINK OF CREATIVITY, WE OFTEN IMAGINE painters, poets, and other traditional artists. This assumes that creativity belongs to the realm of the arts, however, it is far more expansive. It's a vital tool for navigating the ever-changing currents of life. In a world where technology constantly reshapes how we live, communicate, and plan for the future, creativity becomes essential. It's not just about responding to what's in front of us but rather imagining what could be and daring to create a path toward it.

Creativity is a mindset, a lens through which we can view our lives with fresh perspectives. It allows us to move beyond the present moment and envision new possibilities. When we embrace creativity, we stop merely reacting to life and begin actively shaping it. It helps us address immediate challenges but more importantly, it gives us the power to dream bigger and manifest ideas that don't yet exist. This is how meaningful change happens, not just in moments of inspiration but through a continual practice of thinking creatively about who we are and what we can become.

At its heart, creativity is the ability to bring something new into existence, whether that's solving a problem, rethinking an approach to a goal, or discovering a fresh perspective. Yet too often, life's routines pull us away from this kind of thinking. We get caught in the cycle of "to-do lists" and habit, moving through our days as if we are on autopilot. We convince ourselves, "I don't have time," or, "I'm too busy." Before we know it, we've forgotten the power of creativity that lies just beneath the surface of everyday life.

The artist Norman Lewis, known for his abstract expressionist work, once said, "The goal of the artist is to honestly reflect the society in which he lives and to create art that will stimulate the imagination and reflect the truth." This sentiment isn't limited to painting or sculpture. It speaks to the power of creativity in every aspect of life. Whether we're addressing a personal challenge or a professional opportunity, creativity allows us to reflect on our reality and reimagine what is possible, stimulating new ideas that lead to growth. Lewis understood that creativity is not just about creating something beautiful. It's about reflecting deeply on the world around you and finding ways to move it forward.

I've fallen into the trap of routine myself many times. When I first started working on this book, I hit a creative block. The more I sat at my desk, staring at the blank screen, the more stuck I felt. It wasn't until I decided to change my surroundings that things started to shift. One day, I packed up my laptop and went to a café. Watching people go about their lives, the energy of a different environment sparked something in me. Suddenly I wasn't just writing, I was connecting to the creative flow. A small change, a different perspective, unlocked new ideas and renewed my motivation.

That's the beauty of creativity. It doesn't require grand gestures or major life changes. Sometimes a simple shift such as working from a new location, taking a walk instead of sitting at a desk, or trying something different can open the door to new insights. It's about being willing to experiment, to step out of the familiar patterns and see what happens. Small creative changes can lead to big shifts in how we approach our goals, our relationships, and even ourselves.

Creativity is not limited to traditional artistic expression. It weaves into every choice we make, from how we solve daily challenges to how we plan our futures. It allows us to break free from the constraints of habit and rethink the assumptions we've been carrying with us for years. When we approach life creatively, we give ourselves permission to expand our thinking and explore new possibilities we might not have otherwise considered.

One of the most important lessons I've learned about creativity is that it doesn't belong to a special moment or specific talent. It's available to all of us, all the time. We're making creative decisions every day, whether we realize it or not in how we plan our schedules, navigate relationships, or solve problems. The potential for creativity is present in every choice if we allow ourselves to think beyond the conventional and imagine what could be.

Living a creative life means breaking away from routines and embracing the unknown. It's about challenging the limits we've set for ourselves and seeing where new ideas might take us. It requires questioning our first instincts and remaining open to alternatives. Often the boundaries we place on ourselves are the result of habit, not truth. When we cultivate creativity, we begin to see beyond those limitations and in doing so, we provide space for growth, learning, and transformation.

When I look back at the moments of growth in my life, creativity has always been the underlying force. It's what helps us shift perspectives, embrace new experiences, and reinvent ourselves when the familiar no longer serves us. Creativity opens the door to possibility and with it, the chance to live a life that is not only fulfilling but deeply meaningful.

In a world that's constantly evolving, creativity is no longer a luxury but rather essential. It's what allows us to navigate change with grace, to see opportunities where others see obstacles, and to turn ordinary moments into transformative experiences. By adopting a creative mindset, we can shape not just our futures but the very way we move through life.

9

The Strength of Accountability: Owning Your Space

Do the best you can until you know better. Then when you know better, do better.
Maya Angelou

ACCOUNTABILITY, FOR ME, IS ABOUT OWNING MY TRUTHS. I take full responsibility for my actions and the consequences they bring. It's more than just admitting when I've done something wrong. It's about recognizing my choices and understanding their ripple effects, both in my life and in the lives of others. At its core, accountability means holding myself to a standard of integrity. No excuses and no shifting blame.

One lesson I've come to understand is that accountability shapes both personal growth and the depth of my relationships. For instance, when I commit to attending a friend's important event, I make it a priority to show up. I recognize that my presence matters. If something comes up that prevents me from being there, I don't let it slide. I communicate promptly, take responsibility for my absence, and find ways to make up for it. This builds trust and demonstrates that I value our connection. On the flip side, I still recall a childhood memory of a teammate whose excitement was crushed when his father promised to show up at one of our games but never came. That disappointment stayed with me, reinforcing the importance of being reliable and following through.

Accountability, however, isn't just about showing up. It's also about how I respond to my own setbacks. I've learned that maintaining a growth mindset is key to staying accountable. When I fail at something—whether it's missing a deadline or falling short on a personal goal—I don't see it as the end. Instead, I try to treat it as a learning moment. For example, after missing a deadline on a project I was working on, I didn't just sit in regret. I took a step back and asked myself where I went wrong. I reached out to a friend with more experience, seeking feedback that helped me identify what to improve for next time. In doing so, I transformed a mistake into a stepping stone.

Another critical piece of accountability is setting clear expectations. When my goals are vague, it's easy to let things slide. When I outline exactly what I want to achieve—whether it's sticking to a fitness routine or committing more time to family—it becomes easier to track my progress and hold myself to it. For example, when I commit to exercising three times a week, I mark it in my calendar like an important appointment. This makes it more real and harder to ignore. There's something about seeing a task laid out in front of me that makes me more motivated to follow through.

What I've also come to appreciate is that accountability is not an individual pursuit but rather is deeply tied to the community I keep. Over time, I've fostered mutual accountability with my friends and family. We regularly check in on each other's personal goals, which not only holds us accountable but also encourages collective growth. For instance, a close friend and I have a weekly ritual where we share our goals and celebrate even the smallest wins. This camaraderie reminds us that we are not walking this journey alone. We're pushing each other toward our best selves.

Accountability then becomes more than just a responsibility. It's the privilege of knowing that my choices and actions reflect my character and impact the people around me. It's also about having the opportunity to lift others up by being reliable, supportive, and engaged in their growth as well.

When I reflect on my life, I see that accountability has been one of the most profound drivers of my personal evolution. It's what has helped me stay grounded, push through challenges, and connect more deeply with others. By setting clear expectations for myself, learning from setbacks, and surrounding myself with a community of mutual support, I've cultivated a mindset of accountability that empowers me to pursue my aspirations with integrity and purpose.

Accountability goes beyond simply keeping promises or admitting mistakes. It's about the person I become along the way. It's through this practice that I keep evolving, strengthen trust with others, and move through life with greater purpose and clarity.

10

Shaping Your Future Through Continuous Learning

I never lose. I either win or learn.
Nelson Mandela

"There are two kinds of people in the world: Those who believe their fate is written in the stars, and those who believe they hold the pen." This proverb speaks to the essence of a growth mindset, a belief that we can shape our future through our efforts, choices, and willingness to learn. This mindset, coined and championed by Stanford psychologist Carol Dweck, fundamentally shifts how we approach challenges, setbacks, and opportunities. It asserts that intelligence, talent, and success are not predetermined but cultivated through dedication, perseverance, and resilience.

In contrast to a fixed mindset, which sees traits such as intelligence and ability as static and unchangeable, a growth mindset is rooted in the belief that anything can be improved through intentional effort. This belief unlocks the possibility of personal transformation and professional advancement. Where a fixed mindset limits, a growth mindset empowers.

Let's reflect on a common scenario in sports where naturally gifted athletes who, despite their early promise, lose their competitive edge to those with less talent but more determination. These hard-working athletes, who may not have started as stars, hustle every day to improve their skills, outwork their competition, and eventually claim the top spots. The difference is mindset. The talented athletes may coast on their natural abilities, assuming they'll always come out ahead while the determined ones, with a growth mindset, grind to unlock their full potential. It's a clear example that in many cases hunger and persistence outshine raw talent.

This same dynamic applies to professional and personal life. In today's fast-paced, ever-changing economy, adaptability, resilience, and continuous development are not just assets but rather necessities. A fixed mindset traps us in old patterns, holding us back from realizing our full potential. It says, "This is all there is," and forces us to accept the status quo. A growth mindset, on the other hand, opens us up to new possibilities, showing us that there's always room for improvement and that we have the power to change our trajectory.

Take, for example, growing up in an environment where opportunities are scarce and the expectation for success is low. This environment can foster a fixed mindset where nothing is expected to change and effort feels futile. The cycle continues generation after generation. But what happens when someone begins to see beyond those limitations? What if, through mentorship, networking, or exposure to new ideas, that person begins to believe in the possibility of more? With a shift to a growth mindset, that individual begins to break free from inherited limitations. They realize that they are not bound by their circumstances but are capable of creating their own path.

For me, the key to unlocking my growth mindset was education. Growing up in government housing, I didn't initially understand the power of knowledge and learning. Through my educational journey, I realized that education opened doors far beyond what I'd ever imagined. It expanded my worldview, exposed me to new possibilities, and elevated me to heights I had never thought attainable. It was understanding my growth was within my control that fueled my continued pursuit of self-improvement and success.

A growth mindset is more than just a way of thinking. It's a way of living. It's embodied by traits such as ambition, continuous development, adaptability, and proactivity, all of which are directly tied to career success and personal fulfillment. Individuals who embrace a growth mindset are seen by their peers and managers as resilient, passionate, and willing to learn. These individuals don't shy away from challenges but rather seek them out, knowing that every challenge is an opportunity to grow. This mindset naturally leads to more opportunities, whether it's taking on critical projects, receiving promotions, or simply being entrusted with more responsibility.

Organizations also benefit from cultivating a growth mindset among their employees. In dynamic environments, the adaptability, creativity, and resilience that come from a growth mindset make companies more innovative and agile. Employees who believe in their capacity to grow contribute more fully, bringing new ideas and solutions to the table, helping their organizations evolve and thrive.

A growth mindset goes beyond developing a professional strategy. It's a way of living. It's about welcoming challenges, turning setbacks into lessons, and constantly striving for self-improvement. This mindset empowers us to tap into our true potential, push past perceived limits, and create meaningful change not just in our own lives but the lives of others.

As we reflect on the pillars of success, let us remember that a growth mindset is not a fixed trait but a conscious choice. Every day, we have the opportunity to decide how we approach our challenges. Will we see them as barriers that define us or as stepping stones that propel us forward? By choosing a growth mindset, we choose to take ownership of our journey, believing in the power of effort and the limitless possibilities it creates.

Debriefing

P ART III OF *BE STILL, SAY LESS* FOCUSES ON THE CONCEPT of quiet transformation, delving into how inner-strength can be unlocked for significant personal and professional growth. It emphasizes redefining success, the importance of self-evaluation, and the power of aligning actions with core values. This part shifts from understanding oneself (Part I) and navigating relationships (Part II) to actively shaping one's life and career through inner-work and intentional change.

KEY THEMES

- **Redefining Success:** This pillar emphasizes that success is not a standardized concept but rather a personal definition. It encourages readers to liberate themselves from societal expectations and create their own metrics of success based on personal values and fulfillment.
- **Self-Awareness and Self-Evaluation:** Part III stresses the importance of starting with a thorough self-evaluation. This involves taking time for stillness,

reflecting on feelings, and assessing whether one's life and values align. It highlights that individuals often recognize when something is off and when change is needed.

- **Alignment of Values and Work:** A significant theme is the necessity of aligning core values with one's work and career. It addresses the trap of "golden handcuffs," where individuals stay in unfulfilling jobs for financial security. The section encourages readers to ask themselves if their personal well-being is worth the price they are paying.
- **Core Values vs. Company Philosophy:** It's crucial to evaluate whether a company's values align with one's own. Aspects such as interpersonal dynamics, workplace culture, and the purpose of the work are as important as salary and hours.
- **Disconnect Between Wealth and Happiness:** Part III acknowledges that while society often equates wealth with happiness, there is no direct correlation. It highlights that genuine happiness comes from strong systems for maintaining peace, family, and communication, not just material possessions.
- **Responsibility for Healing:** The section underscores that individuals are responsible for their own healing, both personally and professionally. Resentment or frustration in relationships or careers often stems from unresolved internal issues.
- **Balancing Selflessness and Self-Care:** While selflessness is often seen as a virtue, consistently putting others first can lead to burnout and a diminished sense of self-worth. Prioritizing self-care is essential for mental and emotional health.

- **Authentic Impact vs. Attention:** In the age of social media, there's a focus on attention and followers. True influence is about making a positive, lasting change in the world, however, not just chasing numbers.
- **Crafting Your Own Path:** Ultimately, individuals have the power to design their own lives. This involves trusting oneself, listening to intuition, and aligning actions with values. True success is about living authentically on one's own terms.

Part III is about taking proactive steps toward personal and professional fulfillment. It's about moving from awareness to action, from external definitions of success to internal ones. The section encourages readers to do the following.

- **Define their own success** rather than adhering to societal standards.
- **Engage in deep self-reflection** to understand their values and needs.
- **Make intentional choices** to align their lives and careers with their true selves.
- **Prioritize inner well-being** over external achievements.
- **Create meaningful impact** rather than just seeking attention.

In essence, Part III is a call to take ownership of one's life, unlock inner-strength, and create a transformation that is both profound and lasting.

AFFIRMATION

I am committed to continuous development and self-improvement.

SELF-REFLECTION

Part III of *Be Still, Say Less* focuses on redefining success, self-evaluation, and aligning actions with core values to achieve personal and professional growth. Take some time to reflect on the following questions to dive deeper into these themes and apply them to your own life:

1. Redefining Success:
- What does success truly mean to me? Is my definition of success based on my own values or societal expectations?
- What metrics am I currently using to measure my success? Are these metrics truly fulfilling, or are they driven by external validation?
- If I could design my own definition of success, what would it look like? What would I prioritize?
- Am I chasing a "golden handcuffs" scenario, where financial security is prioritized over personal fulfillment?
- How can I shift my perspective to focus on what genuinely brings me joy and purpose?

2. Self-Awareness and Self-Evaluation:
- When was the last time I took a moment for thorough self-evaluation? What did I discover?
- Am I in tune with my feelings? Do I allow myself to feel them, or do I suppress them?

- Do I recognize when something feels off in my life? What are the signs that I need to make a change?
- Am I living in alignment with my values? Where are there discrepancies between what I value and how I live?
- What steps can I take to create more space for stillness and reflection in my daily life?

3. Alignment of Values and Work:
- Does my current work align with my core values? Why or why not?
- Am I happy in my work? Do I feel a sense of purpose and fulfillment?
- What aspects of my work bring me joy? What aspects drain my energy?
- If I could redesign my work life, what would I change? What steps can I take to move in that direction?
- Am I prioritizing wealth over well-being? Is the price I'm paying worth it?

4. Core Values vs. Company Philosophy:
- Do I know the core values of my company or organization? Do they align with my personal values?
- What is the workplace culture like? Does it support my well-being and growth?
- Are the interpersonal dynamics in my workplace healthy and respectful?
- What is the purpose of the work I do? Does it feel meaningful to me?
- If there is a misalignment, what steps can I take to address it or find a better fit?

5. Disconnect Between Wealth and Happiness:
- Do I equate wealth with happiness? Why or why not?
- What are the things that truly bring me happiness? Are they material possessions or something else?
- Am I prioritizing strong systems for maintaining peace, family, and communication in my life?
- How can I shift my focus from external achievements to internal fulfillment?
- What does true happiness mean to me?

6. Responsibility for Healing:
- Am I taking responsibility for my own healing, both personally and professionally?
- Are there unresolved issues from my past that are affecting my present?
- Where do I feel resentment or frustration in my relationships or career? What might be the underlying causes?
- Am I willing to do the inner work necessary for healing and growth?
- What does healing look like for me?

7. Balancing Selflessness and Self-Care:
- Do I tend to put others' needs before my own? Is this a healthy balance or is it leading to burnout?
- Am I prioritizing self-care? What does self-care look like for me?
- Am I able to say "No" when needed? Do I set healthy boundaries?
- Am I pouring from an empty cup? How can I replenish myself?

- What does valuing myself look like in action?

8. Authentic Impact vs. Attention:
- Am I more focused on seeking attention or making a genuine impact?
- What kind of impact do I want to have on the world?
- How can I shift my focus from appearance to authentic contribution?
- What does meaningful impact look like for me?
- How can I measure impact in a way that is authentic and meaningful?

9. Crafting Your Own Path:
- Do I feel I am in control of designing my own life?
- Am I listening to my intuition? Do I trust myself to make the right decisions?
- Are my actions aligned with my values? How can I better align them?
- What does living authentically on my own terms look like?
- What steps can I take to create the life I truly want?

Overall Reflection:
- What key insights have I gained from Part III?
- What areas of my life need the most attention and change?
- What specific action steps will I take to implement what I've learned?
- How will I hold myself accountable for these changes?
- How will I define my own success going forward?

By reflecting on these questions, you can uncover valuable insights into your current state, identify areas where you can unlock your inner-strength, and create a quiet transformation in your life. Be honest and gentle with yourself during this process, and remember that change takes time and effort.

Part IV

Empowered Presence:
Building Awareness
through Resilience
and Connection

Part IV invites us to think beyond our individual journeys and consider the impact we leave behind. It's about legacy—not just in terms of accomplishments, but in the values we embody, the people we uplift, and the systems we help shape. This section challenges us to expand our vision from personal success to collective contribution. It asks: How are we using our influence, wisdom, and experiences to create something that lasts? Legacy is not reserved for the end of life. It's built in every intentional act, every relationship nurtured, and every truth spoken for the greater good.

1

The Resilience Path: Cultivating Authentic Growth

> *Resilience grounds us through challenges, enabling learning, adaptation, and growth. Without it, personal development stalls.*
> Dr. Thurman E. Webb, Jr.

RESILIENCE IS OFTEN MISUNDERSTOOD AS AN INNATE quality that only a few possess. Research has shown, however, that resilience is not a fixed trait. It's a process that anyone can cultivate, strengthen, and rely on during adversity. Psychologists define resilience as the ability to adapt positively in the face of significant stress, adversity, or trauma. Far from being an elusive trait, resilience involves behaviors, thoughts, and actions that can be developed through experience, practice, and a deeper understanding of oneself and others.

At its core, resilience enables individuals to not only cope with adversity but to grow from it. Studies have demonstrated that resilience is closely linked to psychological well-being and long-term success. According to research by Dr. Ann Masten, a prominent psychologist in the field of resilience, it is an "ordinary magic" that she defines as a common phenomenon arising from basic human adaptive systems. In essence, resilience is not rare or exceptional but rather a natural and integral part of human development built upon the foundations of self-awareness, emotional regulation, and effective coping mechanisms.

THE ROLE OF FAMILY IN RESILIENCE FORMATION

Resilience often begins within the family environment, the first and most influential social space where individuals learn to navigate life. The dynamic within a family significantly impacts how a person develops resilience. Research shows that parental influence, particularly the modeling of coping behaviors, plays a critical role in shaping a child's response to stress and adversity. Psychologist Emmy Werner, in her landmark longitudinal study of children from disadvantaged backgrounds, found that children who had strong, supportive family relationships were much more likely to develop resilience even in the face of significant hardship. Conversely, children from dysfunctional or neglectful environments often struggled more with overcoming challenges later in life.

In families where parents model healthy coping strategies, emotional regulation, and problem-solving skills, children are more likely to internalize these behaviors and apply them in their own lives. This influence extends beyond childhood. Individuals who grew up with resilient role models are often better equipped to handle stress, maintain optimism, and pursue solutions in the face of adversity. Families not only provide emotional support but also establish social, ethical, and moral guidelines that shape how individuals approach challenges. It is through these early interactions that resilience begins to take root.

THE KENNEDY FAMILY: A CASE STUDY IN RESILIENCE

The Kennedy family is often cited as an example of resilience in the face of profound adversity. While their story is celebrated for political success, it is also marked by tragedy. Joseph P. Kennedy Sr., the patriarch, rose from humble Irish immigrant roots to financial and social prominence through strategic investments and a Harvard education. Yet despite their success, the Kennedys experienced repeated personal tragedies. John F. Kennedy was assassinated during his presidency, followed by the assassination of his brother Robert Kennedy just five years later. The family endured further losses, including accidents and untimely deaths.

What makes the Kennedy family particularly notable is their ability to persist and continue their legacy despite these overwhelming hardships. Research in resilience highlights this kind of adaptive capacity, where individuals or groups not only recover from trauma but often emerge stronger and more determined. The Kennedys continued involvement in politics even after such devastating losses illustrates the psychological concept of "post-traumatic growth." This concept is tied to positive psychological change that can occur as a result of struggling with highly challenging circumstances. Post-traumatic growth is often seen in individuals who, like the Kennedys, find meaning and purpose in their experiences of loss, which leads to greater resilience and renewed commitment to their goals.

DR. THURMAN E. WEBB, JR.

PSYCHOLOGICAL MECHANISMS OF RESILIENCE

The capacity for resilience is influenced by several psychological mechanisms. One of the most important is cognitive reframing, or the ability to reinterpret stressful events in a way that reduces their emotional impact. This process involves recognizing that setbacks and failures are part of life and instead of seeing them as insurmountable obstacles, viewing them as opportunities for growth. Carol Dweck's research on growth mindset aligns with this concept, showing that individuals who believe in their ability to improve and adapt are more resilient in the face of adversity. They don't view failure as a permanent state but rather as a stepping stone to greater learning and achievement.

Resilience is bolstered by emotional regulation, which is the ability to manage and process emotions effectively. Studies have shown that individuals who can regulate their emotions, particularly during stressful times, are more likely to maintain resilience. This is tied to the development of self-awareness, which allows individuals to recognize their emotional triggers and respond in ways that promote well-being. For example, mindfulness-based practices have been shown to increase emotional regulation and resilience by helping individuals stay present and nonreactive to negative experiences.

Research by Dr. Martin Seligman, a pioneer in positive psychology, highlights the role of optimism in resilience. Seligman's work shows that resilient individuals maintain a positive outlook even during difficult times as they focus on what can be controlled and what positive outcomes may arise from adversity. This mindset helps sustain motivation and perseverance, both key factors in overcoming obstacles and achieving long-term success.

BUILDING RESILIENCE THROUGH SELF-AWARENESS AND RELATIONSHIPS

Developing resilience starts with increasing self-awareness. Knowing your strengths, understanding your limitations, and recognizing patterns of thought and behavior are critical steps in building resilience. Self-reflection enables you to identify the areas in which you can grow and to develop strategies for overcoming challenges more effectively. This involves not only personal introspection but also seeking feedback from others, which can help reveal blind spots and areas for improvement.

Relationships also play a central role in fostering resilience. Psychologist John Bowlby's Attachment Theory emphasizes the importance of secure relationships in developing emotional resilience. Individuals who have supportive networks—whether family, friends, or mentors—are better equipped to handle life's difficulties. Resilient people often have strong social connections that provide emotional support, guidance, and encouragement during tough times. These relationships offer both a buffer against stress and a source of strength, helping individuals navigate crises more effectively.

RESILIENCE AS A PATH TO AUTHENTIC LIVING AND SUCCESS

Resilience is not just about bouncing back from adversity but rather growing through it. As research shows, resilience can be cultivated and strengthened through self-awareness, emotional regulation, and supportive relationships. Whether you're facing personal challenges, professional setbacks, or difficult life transitions, resilience empowers you to adapt, persevere, and ultimately thrive.

In the broader context of self-awareness and personal growth, resilience is the key to living more authentically and achieving your goals. When you build resilience, you unlock the potential to confront adversity with confidence, maintain hope during difficult times, and inspire those around you. As you continue on your journey toward greater self-understanding, remember that resilience is not a fixed trait but a learned attribute that will empower you to make meaningful changes and live a life of purpose, authenticity, and success.

2

Collaborative Growth: Unlocking Collective Progress

Engaging in collaboration means embracing diverse perspectives and shared goals, which renews our creativity, strengthens our resolve, and fosters a sense of unity and purpose.
Dr. Thurman E. Webb, Jr.

"Individually, we are one drop. Together we are an ocean." These words by the poet, Ryunosuke Satoro, capture the essence of collaboration, a key driver of both individual and collective progress. Collaboration means more than just working alongside others. It's the act of combining our efforts, creativity, and resources to achieve a shared goal. Whether we're assembling a complex piece of furniture or trying to move something as cumbersome as a sleeper sofa, certain tasks are impossible to accomplish alone. In these moments, the value of teamwork becomes clear. But collaboration isn't just about convenience. It's about growth, creativity, and the synergy that emerges when people come together to solve problems and create something greater than what any individual could achieve alone.

In my experience as a licensed therapist, I have seen the profound impact that increasing both individual and collective awareness can have on fostering collaboration. When individuals are more aware of their own strengths, limitations, and needs, they are better equipped to contribute to a group. Similarly, when a group embraces mutual understanding and respect, creativity and cooperation naturally follow. Collaboration flourishes in environments where individuals respect and appreciate one another's unique contributions. In these spaces, ideas become more imaginative, innovative, and transformative because they are nurtured by the collective energy of the group.

True collaboration goes beyond simply dividing tasks but rather involves creating a shared vision and working together to bring it to life. Individual effort is vital but when minds merge, the potential for creativity expands exponentially. This is where collective thinking becomes essential. By pooling diverse perspectives, skills, and experiences, teams often develop solutions and ideas that would be unattainable in isolation. This shift in mindset away from a focus on individual achievement and toward a collective approach not only improves the quality of the work but also enhances the sense of fulfillment that comes from shared success.

To foster such collaboration, it's crucial to establish an environment where respect, trust, and open communication are the foundation. When team members feel heard, valued, and respected, they are more likely to share their ideas freely and take creative risks. This type of environment encourages collective creativity, where the whole becomes greater than the sum of its parts. As each person brings their unique strengths to the table, the result is often something more innovative, powerful, and fulfilling than what any one person could have created alone.

Collaboration isn't just a means to an end. It's a driving force that pushes progress forward. Whether in our professional lives, personal relationships, or communities, long-lasting success and fulfillment come from working together. While individual thinking may spark an idea, it's often the input, feedback, and support of others that bring it to life. The most successful outcomes are rarely the result of one person's efforts. They are built on the combined contributions of many, each bringing their own strengths and perspectives to the table.

At its core, collaboration is more than a tool for achieving goals. It's a way of life. It fosters empathy, mutual respect, and a shared sense of purpose. In personal relationships, for example, collaboration isn't just about compromise but rather building something stronger together. Every conversation, every act of support and understanding, strengthens the bond and creates a foundation that's far more resilient than anything we could achieve alone.

The proverb "If you want to go fast, go alone. If you want to go far, go together" speaks directly to the truth that collaboration allows us to achieve more than we initially imagined by guiding us toward growth and deeper connections. When we nurture our self-awareness while honoring the contributions of others, we unlock the potential for transformative progress. Collaboration becomes a pathway not only for personal growth but for collective success and fulfillment.

Whether in the context of a team project, a community effort, or the broader scope of life, collaboration is the compass that points us toward the best version of ourselves and the world around us. It enables us to move beyond individual limitations and harness the collective power of shared goals, creativity, and connection. By embracing collaboration as a mindset, we make space for deeper relationships, innovative ideas, and a lasting impact that extends far beyond what we could achieve on our own.

3

Clarity Through Communication

> *True communication is about seeking clarity, not influence. It is the art of understanding and being understood, fostering genuine connection over persuasion.*
> Dr. Thurman E. Webb, Jr.

I ONCE DATED A WOMAN WHO TOLD ME I WAS A TERRIBLE communicator. Instead of listening, I dismissed her concerns and unsurprisingly, the relationship ended. In hindsight, the problem was clear: I didn't communicate with her, nor did I listen to her. Effective communication is more than just talking. It's about understanding, actively listening, and responding in a way that acknowledges the other person's perspective. Without this foundation, no relationship can survive. Communication is the oxygen of any connection, whether personal or professional. It is the process by which we exchange not just words but emotions, intentions, and ideas. Progress in any relationship isn't just a result of talking but rather truly understanding one another through meaningful dialogue. This idea applies not only to our romantic lives but also to how we engage with the world around us.

The ability to express ourselves clearly and authentically is fundamental to personal growth and understanding. When we learn to communicate effectively, we bridge the gap between our emotions and intellect, opening a channel for self-discovery. For instance, writing in a journal or openly discussing a difficult experience with a trusted friend allows us to process our thoughts and emotions, helping us gain insight into our behavior and patterns. This kind of self-expression brings clarity to who we are at our core.

Yet for many of us, communicating our true feelings or desires isn't easy. Our ability to express ourselves is often shaped by societal norms or learned behaviors from our upbringing. Growing up in an environment where emotions weren't discussed, for example, can make it difficult to show vulnerability as adults. I remember as a kid, a boy could fall off the monkey bars and break his arm but if he cried, we'd call him a sissy. We were told to "Walk it off" or "Eub some dirt on it." The message was clear: Don't show pain, and never show weakness.

Breaking through these barriers to become a more effective communicator can be transformative. Whether through speaking, writing, or nonverbal cues, learning to express ourselves opens up new avenues for personal growth. In our personal lives, clear and assertive communication about our needs creates healthier relationships. Imagine having a disagreement with a close friend. If you avoid the conversation, resentment builds. But if you communicate your feelings while listening to theirs, you can address the issue and strengthen the bond. Similarly, sharing your aspirations with a mentor can open doors for growth and opportunities that you might not have seen on your own.

Effective communication also involves understanding how our environment, cultural backgrounds, and societal influences shape our interactions. For example, having a conversation with a friend from a different culture can deepen your understanding of how language and communication styles influence perspectives. This awareness not only increases your self-awareness but also fosters empathy, allowing you to communicate more effectively with others.

Active listening is a critical component of communication. When you engage deeply in conversations with friends, family, or colleagues, you create a sense of belonging and inclusion. People feel valued when they are truly heard, and this encourages more open, honest dialogue. For instance, if a friend seems upset, asking how they're feeling and genuinely listening to their response creates a safe space for them to share their emotions. This strengthens the connection and builds trust, improving the quality of the relationship.

It's important to remember that communication is not just about talking. It's about listening, understanding, and reflecting. It's about sharing not just words but also emotions and ideas in an authentic way. In both personal and professional settings, people who communicate clearly and honestly tend to have stronger relationships and often find greater success in achieving their goals.

As one of my mentors used to say, "We are valued by the number of lives we touch each day." This highlights the importance of meaningful communication. Whether it's resolving a conflict with a partner or simply sharing your thoughts in a conversation, effective communication allows us to make a positive impact on others while deepening our understanding of ourselves.

Communication goes beyond vocabulary and speech. It includes nonverbal cues, body language, and written expression.

Mastering these skills is essential for navigating personal, social, and professional environments. Clear communication is the foundation upon which we share our ideas, state our needs, and express our feelings. Without it, our goals and expectations remain misunderstood, and progress stalls.

Strong communicators are better positioned in both personal and professional realms because they can articulate their thoughts and feelings with clarity and confidence. They create environments where people feel engaged, valued, and included. This not only leads to better relationships but also encourages the kind of deep, productive conversations that foster mutual growth and understanding.

In a conversation, the goal is not just to share your perspective but to create a dialogue where everyone feels heard and respected. Engaging participants actively as both speakers and listeners fosters a sense of inclusion and importance. When people are prepared and comfortable, conversations flow naturally, allowing for the exchange of meaningful ideas. This in turn encourages personal growth, as everyone involved feels connected, understood, and supported.

This person-centered approach emphasizes the intrinsic value of every participant's contribution. By creating an atmosphere where individuals feel safe to express themselves, we not only increase self-awareness but also promote empathy, active listening, and meaningful personal growth. When we are attuned to others' emotions and perspectives, we foster deeper connections that enhance the quality of our relationships and communication.

The Latin root of the word "communication" is "comunicare," meaning "to share" or "to unite." Communication is fundamentally about connection. Effective communication is not easy. I've known engineers who could design skyscrapers with impeccable precision but struggled to communicate their ideas, stalling their careers. I've seen leaders who were kind to their pets at home but harsh with their employees, showing a disconnect between how they managed their emotions in different environments..

Communication is not just a skill but rather a gateway to deeper self-awareness. It helps us tune into our own thoughts and emotions while forming meaningful connections with others. When we communicate well, we nurture personal growth, strengthen relationships, and cultivate empathy and authenticity in every exchange. Mastering this art gives us the ability to transform not only ourselves but also the world we interact with.

4

The Power of Empowerment

Empowerment is the spark that ignites self-renewal.
It fuels our inner-strength, rejuvenates our spirit, and
propels us toward our true potential.
Dr. Thurman E. Webb, Jr.

EMPOWERMENT IS OFTEN SPOKEN ABOUT BUT RARELY fully understood. At its core, empowerment is about recognizing your own ability to make decisions and take control of your life. It's the process of gaining the confidence and tools to act with competence and independence, especially in challenging situations. Empowerment isn't something external that's given to you. It's an internal shift where you begin to see yourself as capable, resourceful, and in control of your own journey.

In a world that's constantly changing, filled with growing demands and unexpected challenges, empowerment becomes essential. It allows you to thrive, not just survive. Empowerment isn't just about professional success or achieving external goals but rather cultivating self-awareness and fostering a deep sense of purpose. When supported by mentorship, guidance, and psychological empowerment, it becomes a powerful tool for personal growth, mental well-being, and authentic living.

EMPOWERMENT AND PERSONAL GROWTH

To understand empowerment, let's start with what it means in day-to-day life. Empowerment is about feeling capable of handling whatever life throws your way. It's the belief that you can make decisions, influence outcomes, and respond to challenges with confidence. Think of times when you've felt confident in your ability to solve a problem or make an important decision. That's empowerment in action. On the flip side when you feel stuck, unsure, or overwhelmed, it often comes from a place of disempowerment where you don't feel in control or capable of making an impact.

Empowerment is about developing this sense of control and confidence over time. It's not a one-time achievement but a continuous process of self-discovery and growth. Psychological empowerment, specifically, refers to increasing your belief in your own ability to shape your life and influence your environment. When you feel empowered, you approach situations with a proactive mindset, knowing that you have the internal resources to navigate difficulties and pursue your goals.

For example, if you've ever felt nervous about speaking up in a meeting but did so anyway because you knew your perspective was valuable, that's empowerment. It's not about eliminating fear but recognizing your worth and acting despite it. This kind of empowerment enhances your sense of self-determination, leading to greater satisfaction and personal achievement.

THE ROLE OF MENTORSHIP IN EMPOWERMENT

Mentorship plays a crucial role in fostering empowerment. A supportive mentor acts as both a guide and a cheerleader, helping you recognize your potential and providing you with the tools to succeed. Mentors offer not only practical advice but also emotional support, encouraging you to step outside your comfort zone and trust your abilities.

Imagine having a mentor who believes in you even when you doubt yourself. Their confidence in your potential can inspire you to take risks, embrace challenges, and grow in ways you might not have thought possible. Through their guidance, you begin to see your own strengths more clearly, gaining the confidence to tackle obstacles and pursue your ambitions.

As previously discussed, mentorship doesn't have to be formal. It can come from various relationships in your life. Whether it's a teacher, a colleague, or a trusted friend, having someone who supports your growth and pushes you to see your own power is invaluable.

EMPOWERMENT THROUGH SELF-AWARENESS

A significant part of empowerment is self-awareness. You can't fully step into your power without understanding who you are knowing your strengths, weaknesses, fears, and desires. Self-awareness is the foundation of empowerment because it allows you to act in alignment with your true self.

Cultivating self-awareness involves regularly reflecting on your thoughts, emotions, and actions. This could mean taking time each day to journal, meditate, or simply think about how you're feeling and why. Over time, these practices help you identify patterns in your behavior and responses, giving you the insight needed to make more intentional choices.

When you know yourself well, you're better equipped to handle challenges. You can recognize when you're feeling overwhelmed and take steps to care for yourself. You can see opportunities for growth and push yourself to step outside your comfort zone. Empowerment through self-awareness means living in tune with your authentic self rather than being controlled by external pressures or fears.

THE IMPORTANCE OF COPING STRATEGIES

Feeling empowered doesn't mean never facing difficulties but rather developing the tools to navigate challenges effectively. Coping strategies are a vital part of empowerment, as they allow you to handle stress, adapt to change, and stay resilient in the face of adversity.

Coping strategies can take many forms ranging from physical activities such as exercise and deep breathing to mental practices including mindfulness and positive self-talk. These techniques help you manage your emotional responses so that even in difficult moments, you feel equipped to stay calm and make thoughtful decisions. By practicing coping strategies regularly, you build mental resilience that in turn strengthens your sense of empowerment.

Empowerment also involves recognizing that it's okay to ask for help. Whether it's leaning on friends, seeking advice from a mentor, or talking to a therapist, knowing when to reach out for support is a sign of strength, not weakness.

EMPOWERMENT IN RELATIONSHIPS AND COMMUNITIES

Empowerment isn't something that happens in isolation. It thrives in relationships and communities where people uplift and support one another. Building positive, supportive relationships can significantly enhance your sense of empowerment. When you surround yourself with people who believe in you, you're more likely to believe in yourself.

Empowered individuals also naturally empower those around them. When you feel confident and in control of your own life, you're more willing and able to support others in their journey. This creates a ripple effect because as you empower yourself, you empower others, leading to collective growth and success.

Whether you're working on a team, building a community, or nurturing a personal relationship, empowerment deepens connections and fosters collaboration. Empowered individuals contribute to an environment where everyone can thrive, offering encouragement, sharing resources, and celebrating each other's successes.

PRACTICAL TIPS FOR CULTIVATING EMPOWERMENT

Empowerment can be cultivated through intentional actions and practices. Here are a few strategies to increase your sense of empowerment and live more authentically:

- **Seek Supportive Mentors:** Find people who inspire you, challenge you, and believe in your potential. Their guidance can help you navigate challenges and grow.
- **Cultivate Self-Awareness:** Spend time reflecting on your thoughts, emotions, and behaviors. Journaling or mindfulness practices can help you get in touch with your inner-self.
- **Set Clear Goals:** Define personal goals that align with your values and passions. Achieving these goals will boost your confidence and sense of accomplishment.
- **Develop Coping Strategies:** Practice techniques that help you manage stress, such as meditation, exercise, or breathing exercises. These will strengthen your mental resilience.
- **Build Positive Relationships:** Surround yourself with people who uplift and support you. Strong relationships enhance your sense of belonging and empowerment.
- **Engage in Lifelong Learning:** Stay curious and open to new ideas. Continuous learning helps you stay adaptable and empowered in a constantly changing world.

EMPOWERMENT AS A LIFELONG JOURNEY

Empowerment is not a destination but rather a lifelong journey of self-discovery, growth, and authenticity. It's about recognizing your own strength, trusting your abilities, and making decisions that align with your values. When you embrace empowerment, you open the door to living a more fulfilling, authentic life.

The more empowered you become, the more you inspire

those around you to step into their own power. Whether through mentorship, self-awareness, or fostering positive relationships, empowerment is a pathway to personal success, collective growth, and a deeper connection to your true self. In the end, living authentically and empowered means recognizing that you have the ability to shape your life, influence the world around you, and uplift others.

5

Setting and Maintaining Healthy Boundaries

> *Setting boundaries and owning your space is an act of self-respect and empowerment. It protects your energy, honors your needs, and allows you to thrive authentically.*
> Dr. Thurman E. Webb, Jr.

I ONCE WORKED WITH A HIGH-PERFORMING EXECUTIVE who had a firm rule: No meetings before 9 a.m. He was meticulous about his morning routine, using the early hours for exercise, reflection, and planning his day. He knew that jumping straight into meetings first thing in the morning drained his energy and clouded his thinking. This was a non-negotiable boundary for him but it wasn't always easy to uphold, especially in a fast-paced corporate environment where early meetings were common.

In his new role, he felt pressure to accommodate his team and clients, often agreeing to 7 a.m. or 8 a.m. meetings despite knowing they threw off his rhythm. While he wanted to foster connection and maintain his reputation as a team player, the early starts left him exhausted and less focused. Over time, he realized that he wasn't contributing as effectively as he could. His conversations lacked depth and his interactions felt forced because he wasn't fully present.

After some reflection, he decided to have an honest conversation with his leadership team. To his surprise, they were understanding and supportive of his need to protect his mornings. His manager even admitted to preferring late-morning meetings herself but had never thought to express it. This simple conversation allowed him to reset his boundaries and honor his natural energy levels, resulting in more productive meetings and a greater sense of alignment between his work and personal priorities.

This experience reinforced the importance of recognizing personal limits and communicating them clearly. By setting boundaries, he was able to show up more authentically and contribute in a more meaningful way. It's a reminder that honoring your needs not only benefits you but can also enhance the quality of your work and relationships.

This story highlights a fundamental truth: Having the energy to meet the moment is essential for being fully present and engaged with life's opportunities and challenges. When we push ourselves past our limits, we cheat ourselves and those around us. Our interactions become less genuine, our contributions less meaningful, and our experiences less fulfilling. To truly honor each moment, we must recognize and cultivate the energy required to be fully present. This often means setting boundaries to protect that energy.

By establishing and respecting our own boundaries, we maintain the vitality needed to bring our best selves to every situation, enriching both our lives and the lives of those we interact with.

This practice isn't about being selfish or rigid but rather knowing when we are at our best and making choices that support our long-term well-being.

BOUNDARIES AS A FOUNDATION FOR SUCCESS

Society often glorifies the hustle, the idea that working harder, dreaming bigger, and constantly striving for more is the only path to success. It can feel like the people who win are the ones willing to sacrifice their mental and emotional health to get ahead. The reality is quite different. Some of the most accomplished individuals, from Michelle Obama to Warren Buffet, believe in the power of setting boundaries. They understand that protecting your time and energy is an essential component of success.

Setting boundaries is not only a practice in self-care but also an act of self-awareness. It requires reflection on what truly matters to you and the courage to communicate those needs to others. Boundaries aren't about saying "No" to opportunities but rather saying "Yes" to what's most important in your life—your well-being, relationships, and peace of mind. The misconception that success must come at the cost of our health and happiness is just that—a misconception. True success includes balance, fulfillment, and the ability to be present in the moments that matter most.

NAVIGATING BOUNDARIES IN PERSONAL RELATIONSHIPS

It's not just in professional settings that boundaries play a crucial role. In personal relationships, people also often struggle to set limits. They feel compelled to be constantly available to attend every social event, answer every message, and stay up late to accommodate others. They justify this behavior by saying, "I care so much about these relationships that it doesn't feel like a burden." In reality, this lack of boundaries can lead to burnout and resentment.

It's common to fear missing out on meaningful interactions. As a result, we stretch ourselves thin, telling ourselves we can rest later. The truth is that without boundaries, our interactions become shallow, and we're not really present. Learning to say, "This is my schedule today, and I can't stay out late," is not about rejecting relationships. It's about ensuring that when we do engage, it's with our full energy and authenticity.

THE UNIQUE CHALLENGES OF HIGH ACHIEVERS

Overachievers and perfectionists, often called "high producers," face a specific set of challenges when it comes to setting boundaries. They are driven by their desire to excel, often at the expense of their personal lives. High producers are the ones who work late into the night, convinced that more effort will yield better results. In their pursuit of success, they often lose sight of the balance needed for a fulfilling life.

For these individuals, setting boundaries can feel counterintuitive. They may not realize they're neglecting family time or personal needs until someone points it out. Even then, they might struggle to change their habits. Finding a healthy balance between work and personal life is crucial for maintaining long-term success. High achievers who set boundaries not only improve their personal well-being but also enhance their professional performance. When they allow themselves time to rest and recharge, they return to their work with greater clarity, creativity, and focus.

THE IMPORTANCE OF TIME MANAGEMENT

At the heart of setting boundaries is effective time management. Boundaries help define expectations, and time management ensures those boundaries are respected. For instance, managers may expect employees to be flexible during a crisis, but high producers should recognize the difference between occasional overtime and a habit of overworking. Consistently stretching employees beyond their limits leads to burnout and diminishing returns.

Boundaries aren't a sign of weakness but rather an indicator of wisdom and self-awareness. They empower us to define our priorities, protect our well-being, and nurture meaningful relationships. By cultivating healthy boundaries, we create space for a life filled with achievements, balance, and personal growth. High producers who learn to set boundaries will find that they can still accomplish great things without sacrificing what matters most.

Boundaries are ultimately about safeguarding the energy required to show up authentically and fully in each moment. By preserving our time and protecting our well-being, we make sure that we can engage with the world as our best selves, enhancing not only our own lives but also those of the people around us.

6

The Essential Strength of Empathy

Through empathy, we connect more authentically with others and ourselves.
Dr. Thurman E. Webb, Jr.

IN ANY PURSUIT—PERSONAL, PROFESSIONAL, OR ACADEMIC— emotional regulation and empathy are essential for a fulfilling life. While rational thinking is often emphasized as the key to navigating challenges, balancing sensitivity with logic allows us to adapt more successfully. Empathy and emotional intelligence aren't just complementary skills. They are essential for building authentic relationships, especially in a world where digital interactions can hinder connection.

Empathy fosters more than just effective communication. It enables deeper, human-centered solutions. As artificial intelligence takes on more complex tasks, creativity and empathy remain distinctly human and irreplaceable. Machines can process data, but they lack the ability to connect with the emotional layers of human experiences. This makes empathy a critical trait for those seeking to thrive in today's fast-paced and increasingly automated world.

EMPATHY: A CATALYST FOR GROWTH

Empathy is fundamental to personal growth and effective communication. It allows us to relate to others and foster a deeper understanding in our interactions, whether with family, friends, or colleagues. In today's diverse, interconnected society, empathy is more than a nice-to-have trait. It's essential. The ability to understand and respond to others' emotions leads to richer, more meaningful relationships and helps navigate differences with respect and openness.

Many assume empathy is innate, but it is a skill that can be developed. It involves not just understanding another's feelings but also acting with consideration and compassion. Cultivating empathy leads to benefits such as improved cooperation, stronger teamwork, and effective communication. It enhances leadership, supports personal connections, and promotes a more tolerant, respectful environment.

THE SCIENCE OF EMPATHY

Empathy engages the mirror neurons in our brains, allowing us to experience and resonate with the emotions of others. This neural mirroring fosters a profound sense of interconnectedness, making it easier to relate to and support each other. By honing empathy, we become more present and attentive in our interactions, enhancing not only our relationships but also our self-awareness and emotional resilience.

Empathy enables us to bridge divides, helping us move from

judgment to understanding. It promotes mindfulness, enriching our everyday interactions and leading to personal growth as we expand our perspectives and deepen our appreciation for the human experience.

EMPATHY IN RELATIONSHIPS AND LEADERSHIP

Empathy is key to fostering productive and fulfilling relationships, both personally and professionally. It drives effective interactions, enhances creativity, and accelerates personal development. Empathetic leaders build trust and loyalty, creating environments where people feel valued and supported. This in turn fosters stronger teams and more innovative problem-solving.

In a world that often emphasizes efficiency, empathy can seem rare yet it is crucial for building lasting, meaningful connections. Cultivating empathy improves our ability to navigate difficult conversations, support others, and lead with integrity.

EMPATHY AND SUCCESS

Despite its importance, empathy is often overlooked in advice about success. Emotional intelligence and empathy are sometimes dismissed as "soft skills," yet they are increasingly essential for thriving in both personal and professional spheres. Recognizing the need for empathy allows us to foster deeper relationships and communicate more effectively.

Cultivating empathy not only contributes to personal success but also helps build a more compassionate and interconnected world. It reshapes how we interact with others, enhancing our ability to lead, connect, and nurture meaningful relationships. True success isn't just about accomplishments. It's reflected in the richness of our connections and the strength of our relationships. Empathy is more than just a skill. It's a way of living. It brings depth to our lives and those around us, paving the way for deeper fulfillment and a more meaningful form of success.

7

The Vital Practice of Self-Care

Self-care is not a luxury but a necessity.
Dr. Thurman E. Webb, Jr.

S ELF-CARE IS MORE THAN JUST A TRENDY BUZZWORD. IT'S A deeply intentional practice rooted in self-awareness. It involves understanding your physical, emotional, and mental needs and then acting on that understanding to nurture your overall well-being. Many people associate self-care with activities such as going to a spa or indulging in a favorite meal. While these can be enjoyable aspects of self-care, the real power lies in a deeper, more thoughtful process that starts with self-awareness and grows into consistent, purposeful action.

THE ROLE OF SELF-AWARENESS IN SELF-CARE

Self-awareness is the cornerstone of effective self-care. Without a clear understanding of your own needs, stressors, and habits, it's impossible to genuinely care for yourself. Consider someone who feels constantly overwhelmed at work. They might think a weekend getaway or a night out with friends will alleviate their stress but without addressing the root cause, that temporary relief won't last. The real issue might be setting better boundaries at work or confronting feelings of inadequacy. Self-care that truly works begins with understanding what's driving the stress beneath the surface.

In my own life, self-awareness became the turning point when I noticed how certain activities drained my energy. I realized that spending too much time on social media left me feeling anxious and unfocused. Initially, I brushed it off as a minor annoyance but over time, I saw the toll it took on my mood and productivity. Once I acknowledged this, I made conscious changes by limiting my social media use and engaging in more fulfilling activities such as reading and taking walks. By becoming aware of how certain habits impacted my well-being, I could create a self-care routine that genuinely supported my mental health.

RECOGNIZING PATTERNS AND ADJUSTING BEHAVIORS

Self-awareness also helps us recognize patterns in how we respond to stress, disappointment, or life's challenges. A friend of mine used to feel constantly drained because she never set limits. She said "Yes" to every social event, helped others without hesitation, and tried to meet all expectations. It wasn't until she reached the point of emotional burnout that she realized how deeply she was neglecting her own needs. Through journaling and self-reflection, she learned to prioritize herself by saying "No" more often and giving herself guilt-free downtime. This shift wasn't easy, but it was essential for her well-being.

Her experience highlights an important truth: Self-care is about more than occasional indulgence. It requires setting boundaries, listening to your own needs, and making deliberate choices that protect your energy. This kind of self-care emerges from self-awareness—knowing when to say "No," recognizing your limits, and acting in ways that preserve your emotional and mental health.

EMOTIONAL AWARENESS AND HEALTHY COPING MECHANISMS

Emotional self-care is another crucial aspect of this journey. When we ignore our emotions they tend to build up, often leading to unhealthy coping mechanisms. Self-awareness helps us recognize emotional triggers and create healthier responses. For example, someone might notice that after a stressful day, they turn to comfort foods or binge-watch TV as a distraction. Over time, this behavior might lead to physical discomfort or emotional stagnation. A more self-aware approach would involve recognizing this pattern and addressing the underlying feelings. Instead of turning to distractions, they might find relief through journaling, a walk, or talking to a trusted friend. This shift in approach transforms self-care from a reactive response to a proactive, intentional practice.

I recall a time when I felt overwhelmed by responsibilities both at work and home. My instinct was to push through, believing that if I just kept going, things would eventually improve. This only left me feeling more exhausted. When I finally paused and reflected, I realized I was ignoring my own need for rest and balance. I wasn't taking the time to recharge, and it was taking a toll on my mental and physical health. Once I became aware of this, I made small but meaningful changes by carving out quiet time each morning, prioritizing sleep, and learning to delegate tasks. These adjustments didn't solve everything overnight, but they led to a sustainable, meaningful form of self-care that supported my well-being in the long run.

THE IMPACT OF ENVIRONMENTS AND RELATIONSHIPS ON WELL-BEING

Self-awareness also extends to understanding how our environments and relationships impact our energy. Many of us have experienced situations where we feel drained after spending time with certain people or in particular settings. This can be a sign that boundaries need to be set or that we need to limit exposure to negative influences. A friend of mine found that her social circle, while fun and lively, left her emotionally depleted. She realized she was often giving more than she received in those relationships and it was affecting her well-being. By becoming more aware of how these dynamics impacted her, she made the difficult decision to step back from certain friendships. This allowed her to focus on relationships that felt more balanced and supportive, which was an essential step in her self-care journey.

SELF-AWARENESS AND LONG-TERM SELF-CARE

Self-care and self-awareness are fundamentally linked. Without a clear understanding of your own needs, genuine self-care becomes elusive. That understanding comes from taking time for reflection, being honest with yourself, and practicing mindfulness. By tuning in to your emotional, mental, and physical well-being, you can make intentional choices that truly nurture your health. This could mean establishing boundaries, saying "No" when necessary, or engaging in activities that truly nourish your spirit.

Self-care is not about doing what feels good in the moment but rather making conscious choices that support your long-term health and happiness. By cultivating self-awareness, you deepen your understanding of yourself, which allows you to take better care of yourself. This process requires patience and consistency, but it's one of the most valuable investments you can make. Through self-awareness and intentional self-care, you create a life that feels balanced, fulfilling, and true to who you are.

8

The Role of Self-Reflection in Growth

Self-reflection turns experience into wisdom.
Dr. Thurman E. Webb, Jr.

SELF-REFLECTION IS THE PROCESS OF EVALUATING YOUR experiences, goals, values, attitudes, behaviors, and motivations. It offers an opportunity to deeply assess your strengths and weaknesses, enabling you to make meaningful changes and reinforce positive qualities. More than a passive activity, it's an intentional practice that requires thoughtful observation and a heightened consciousness of your thoughts, words, and actions.

At its core, self-reflection is about bending the light of our experiences inward to gain insight. In the same way light reflects in the opposite direction when bent, self-reflection allows us to look back at our inner-world with clarity and purpose. This process combines introspection, meditation, and self-questioning to help us make decisions aligned with our values, strengths, and true needs. People who regularly engage in self-reflection tend to experience greater personal and professional fulfillment as they develop a sense of control and direction in their lives.

THE INTENTIONALITY OF SUCCESS

Personal and professional success is intentional. This may sound simplistic, but it's a powerful truth. Living a meaningful life requires making thoughtful choices and facing challenges head-on. Part of this process involves engaging in honest self-reflection, which requires asking yourself the hard questions about your behaviors, decisions, and motivations. This practice is what matures us, allowing us to navigate life more effectively.

Self-reflection isn't just a tool for solving problems, though it certainly can help with that. It is a practice of stepping back from immediate experiences to learn, meditate, and gain personal insight. This distance from the everyday grind allows us to reflect on both our positive and negative encounters, using them as stepping stones for growth. By reflecting on our past and present, we gain insights that shape our future. This continuous process of learning from our experiences contributes to long-term personal and professional development.

TURNING KNOWLEDGE INTO WISDOM

Reflection is how we transform information into wisdom. Without it, we may encounter facts and experiences, but they remain disconnected from deeper understanding. Reflection integrates this information, helping us build wisdom over time. It's a practice that should be a part of our daily routines to create space for thought and consideration of our actions, decisions, and beliefs.

When I first started recording my thoughts, it was more of an artistic expression. I simply arranged words that reflected how I felt in the moment. Over time, however, I realized the importance of making this a daily habit. What began as a creative exercise became a tool for self-reflection and growth. I shared with others some of my thoughts, and they resonated with people in unexpected ways. This process taught me that reflection is not about saying something new, but rather re-examining what has already been experienced in a way that brings new understanding. Sometimes, as I learned from being around other creative individuals, you have to live a bit before you can reflect meaningfully. My habit of reflection started there, and it's something I recommend to anyone seeking personal growth.

To center yourself through self-reflection, create a space that allows you to be still and present with your thoughts. This might mean setting aside time each day to journal, meditate, or simply pause and think. Reflection doesn't have to be long or complicated, but it should be intentional.

SELF-REFLECTION IN PROFESSIONAL DEVELOPMENT

Self-reflection plays a critical role in personal growth and professional development. For example, educators developing self-reflection skills can transform their teaching methods. Teachers who engage in regular reflection are more likely to shift toward student-centered techniques and cooperative learning strategies, both of which have been shown to enhance student motivation, comprehension, and retention of knowledge. Self-reflection helps educators improve their practices by understanding their strengths and areas for growth.

New teachers in particular benefit greatly from self-reflection, as it helps them apply theoretical knowledge to real-world teaching scenarios. Reflecting on their professional experiences enables them to adjust their techniques, respond to classroom challenges more effectively, and continue learning from each teaching moment. Moreover, self-reflection fosters peer interaction and encourages spontaneous professional development based on shared experiences and common issues within the educational landscape.

THE BROADER IMPACT OF SELF-REFLECTION

When people hear the term "self-reflection," they might imagine someone sitting quietly, lost in thought, rehashing past experiences. While this is one aspect of the practice, true self-reflection goes beyond passive contemplation. It is a series of intentional exercises that anyone can use to examine their thoughts, behaviors, and feelings. It provides a structured way to analyze our personal characteristics for both growth and emotional intelligence, often with greater clarity than we gain from simply living through experiences.

By regularly practicing self-reflection, we build emotional intelligence, improve our decision-making, and develop a more profound understanding of ourselves. This self-awareness allows us to better navigate personal and professional challenges, leading to more intentional choices and deeper satisfaction in life.

Self-reflection is not just a tool for understanding the past but a compass for the future as well. It enables us to align our actions with our values and helps us cultivate a life that feels both balanced and meaningful. Whether you're seeking to improve in your career, relationships, or personal well-being, self-reflection is an essential practice for growth and fulfillment.

MAKING REFLECTION A HABIT

To truly benefit from self-reflection, it needs to be a consistent part of your routine. Set aside time each day to reflect on your experiences. This practice will help you turn everyday experiences into valuable insights and allow you to make more informed, thoughtful decisions moving forward.

Incorporating self-reflection into your life will lead to more intentional living, deeper personal growth, and greater professional success. It's an investment in yourself that pays off in every area of your life, guiding you toward becoming the best version of yourself and empowering you to make the most of the opportunities life presents.

9

The Art and Practice of Decision-Making

> *Whenever you see a successful business, someone once made a courageous decision.*
> Peter Drucker

OUR PERSONAL QUALITIES, CHARACTERISTICS, AND experiences shape the decisions we make, gradually molding us into experts in our fields. Decision-making is a core part of life. Whether in professional or personal settings, we constantly face choices that require thoughtful consideration. These decisions, both big and small, define our success and fulfillment. The ability to make deliberate, informed decisions, especially in uncertain situations, forms the foundation for long-term success.

At some point, everyone asks themselves, "How can I consistently make decisions that lead to successful outcomes?" The key lies in understanding the strategies experts use when making choices, applying them with courage, and maintaining self-awareness.

THE NATURE OF DECISION-MAKING

Decision-making is the mental process of selecting the best course of action from multiple alternatives. It plays a crucial role in solving problems and planning for the future. Whether we're deciding on financial investments, career moves, or personal relationships, each choice is shaped by our circumstances, goals, and understanding of the situation.

In business, decision-making is often complex due to the high stakes involved. Entrepreneurs and leaders must constantly weigh alternatives to improve services, compete in markets, and manage resources effectively. This process begins with gathering information and carefully evaluating potential outcomes, ensuring that decisions align with both short- and long-term goals. Rushing into decisions without reflection can lead to costly mistakes, while taking the time to assess options generally leads to more successful results. As my mentor once told me, "Webb, there's no such thing as a big decision. They're just decisions that need to be made. Great leaders step up and make them."

DECISION-MAKING AND PERSONAL GROWTH

In both personal and professional contexts, decisions have a profound impact on our lives. Each choice we make contributes to shaping our future. Success, especially in significant projects or challenges, often requires confidence, self-awareness, and the courage to take risks. Whether choosing a career path, managing relationships, or pursuing life goals, thoughtful decision-making plays a pivotal role.

Confidence in decision-making stems from both practice and

self-awareness. For example, when faced with the decision to take on a major project, it's important to consider not only the rewards but also your ability to manage risks. Aligning decisions with your strengths while acknowledging areas for improvement leads to better outcomes.

In my own journey, determination and reflection have been key to making effective decisions. When I started my first business, I faced countless choices such as whether to take on new clients, how to allocate my time, and when to expand. Some decisions required careful planning, while others were more intuitive. Recognizing my strengths in creativity and problem-solving helped guide me, but I also sought advice from mentors to avoid costly mistakes.

EMBRACING RISK AND SELF-AWARENESS

Risk-taking is integral to decision-making, and while some decisions require more courage than others, all benefit from self-awareness. For instance, when I considered a significant investment in a project, the risks felt overwhelming. Rather than rushing into it, I took time to gather information, consult with experts, and reflect on my long-term goals. This process allowed me to move forward confidently, knowing the decision aligned with both my ambitions and my tolerance for risk.

The same principles apply to personal decisions. In one instance, I had to navigate a difficult conversation with a family member. It wasn't just about what to say—it was about how to approach the situation to foster understanding rather than conflict. Taking time to reflect on our relationship and consider both perspectives helped me make a decision that prioritized connection and respect. This experience reinforced the importance of combining emotional awareness with rational decision-making.

Pressure often intensifies decision-making. I remember a time when I had to make a major career change with little time to decide. The stakes were high, and I had to choose between staying in a stable role or pursuing a more passionate but uncertain path. In moments like these, I relied on the values I'd cultivated over time. I asked myself, "What truly matters to me? What will I regret not pursuing?" Choosing the riskier option felt more authentic, and although the journey wasn't easy, it led to greater personal and professional fulfillment.

NAVIGATING AMBIGUITY IN DECISION-MAKING

Life is rarely black and white, and decision-making often involves navigating ambiguity. When choices are unclear or when conflicting priorities arise, personal values and principles become essential. I once faced an ethical dilemma that required me to weigh the potential impact on myself and others. By taking time to reflect on what felt right rather than what was easy, I made a decision aligned with my integrity. In hindsight, the long-term benefits far outweighed the short-term discomfort of the harder choice.

Decision-making isn't always a solitary process. Seeking input from trusted mentors, friends, or colleagues can provide valuable perspectives. While the final decision rests with you, involving others in the process can uncover alternatives or solutions you may not have considered. One of the most valuable lessons I've learned is that decision-making isn't about always being right. It's about learning from the outcomes and making adjustments as necessary.

For example, when I was deciding whether to relocate to a new city, I sought input from both my personal and professional networks. Friends reminded me of the personal connections I had where I was, while professional contacts outlined the potential opportunities in the new city. By weighing these perspectives alongside my own goals, I made a more informed choice that ultimately led to growth in both my personal and professional life.

THE PATH TO SUCCESS THROUGH DECISION-MAKING

Personal success often hinges on the ability to make thoughtful, timely decisions. Each choice we make, whether related to our career, relationships, or daily routines, shapes the path ahead. Success isn't just about sticking to a plan. It's about being adaptable, recognizing your strengths and weaknesses, and knowing when to seek guidance. Decision-making rarely follows a straightforward path, but with self-awareness and a clear sense of your values, you can confidently navigate the complexities of life.

Decisions are powerful tools for growth. Each choice, whether successful or not, is an opportunity to learn and refine your approach. As you continue making decisions, remember that they shape not just your immediate outcomes but also your long-term journey. By developing your decision-making skills, seeking wisdom from others, and trusting your instincts, you can chart a course toward personal and professional success.

10

Goal Setting

> *Difficult takes a day, impossible takes a week.*
> Jay Z

GOALS ARE MORE THAN ASPIRATIONS. THEY ARE THE guiding force that motivates people, shapes their actions, and provides them with a sense of purpose and control. Whether personal or professional, goals serve as a roadmap for growth, driving individuals and organizations toward success. For any organization, the more its members plan for its future, the greater the probability of achieving that future. Setting well-defined, challenging, and measurable goals can prevent the organization from drifting off course, ensuring that efforts remain aligned with long-term objectives. As the saying goes, "What gets measured gets done." Goals, when quantifiable and clearly outlined, create focus and momentum, turning abstract visions into concrete realities.

In the world of competitive sports or the arts, outcome goals are critical to achieving excellence. Consider athletes who aim to swim 25 yards in under 30 seconds or musicians striving to land a lead role in a performance. Such goals motivate not only individuals but entire teams, pushing them to strive for success together. Equally important are process or learning goals, which focus on honing specific skills that lead to long-term success. A basketball player working on perfecting their foot positioning or a tennis player aiming to consistently land their serve in the service box exemplify process goals that support overall performance. These small, focused efforts contribute significantly to larger achievements, showing that success is built on a foundation of continual progress.

For those balancing work and study, having both short- and long-term goals is key. Setting monthly milestones rather than fixating solely on distant objectives makes the journey more manageable and provides motivation along the way. Breaking down long-term goals into smaller, achievable parts gives clarity to the path ahead. By separating larger goals into specific indicators of progress, each step becomes a clear marker of achievement.

PERSONAL AND PROFESSIONAL GOALS

It's important to recognize that goals can be divided into personal and professional categories, both of which are necessary for a well-rounded, fulfilling life. Professional goals provide direction in career advancement, but personal goals often lay the foundation for professional success. In many cases, personal development directly impacts career growth. As you define your professional goals, it's crucial to also define your personal ones. Writing these goals down—whether in a journal or a note on your phone—makes them tangible and reminds you of the steps you need to take to achieve them.

Action is what transforms goals from mere ideas into reality.

Without taking action, goals remain dreams or visions. But when broken into smaller tasks and spread over time, those dreams become achievable. Using a calendar to track the progress of each element of your goal gives you a visual plan and helps maintain your focus. Whether it's completing a degree, building a business, or pursuing personal development, each step moves you closer to your final objective.

BREAKING DOWN BIG DREAMS

Breaking large goals into smaller, attainable parts is key to maintaining momentum. Take climbing Mount Everest as an example: If viewed as a single, monumental task, it can seem overwhelming. But when broken into stages, each leg of the journey becomes more achievable. This approach aligns with Time Warner CEO Glenn Britt's advice: "If your aspirations are greater than your current abilities, don't be discouraged. That's not a fault. That's a motivator."

Research shows that nearly 95% of people use the word "goal" interchangeably with "dream." While it's important to dream big, leaving goals at the dream stage keeps them unattainable. As Steve Jobs famously said, "I'm convinced that about half of what separates the successful entrepreneurs from the nonsuccessful ones is pure perseverance." Setting goals that turn dreams into actionable steps is the cornerstone of any achievement.

THE POETRY OF GOALS: REFLECTIONS FROM AFRICAN AMERICAN POETS

African American poets have long reflected on themes of perseverance, purpose, and self-determination, many of which resonate deeply with the essence of goal-setting. Consider Langston Hughes' poem "Dreams," which urges us to hold fast to our dreams for without them, life becomes barren and unfulfilled: "Hold fast to dreams, For if dreams die Life is a broken-winged bird That cannot fly."

This timeless verse reminds us of the importance of not just dreaming but acting on those dreams, transforming them into goals that give our lives flight. Similarly, Gwendolyn Brooks captures the determination needed to achieve one's vision in her poem "The Ballad of Rudolph Reed," where the protagonist's relentless pursuit of his dreams is a testament to the power of perseverance.

Lucille Clifton also speaks to the resilience necessary in the pursuit of goals in her poem "won't you celebrate with me". Her words reflect the idea that daily perseverance, despite obstacles, contributes to long-term success: "Everyday something has tried to kill me and has failed."

These powerful lines remind us that progress isn't always linear and that persistence in the face of difficulty is crucial to achieving any goal.

ADJUSTING COURSE

It's important to note that goals are not rigid. Sometimes, after working toward a goal, we may realize it's not realistic or no longer aligned with our current aspirations. Periodically reviewing your progress is essential to determining whether your goals still serve you. Adjusting your strategies or even the goals themselves is part of the journey toward success. If a particular approach isn't bringing you closer to your objective, consider a new course of action. Flexibility is as important as persistence in achieving long-term success.

GOALS AS THE KEY TO SUCCESS

Setting clear, actionable goals is a key to unlocking success. They provide the focus, motivation, and direction needed to navigate challenges and strive toward personal and professional fulfillment. Goals transform aspirations into achievable outcomes, while also fostering accountability by helping individuals track their progress, refine their approach, and remain dedicated in the face of obstacles. As the saying goes, "A goal without a plan is just a wish." By embracing goal-setting, people lay the foundation for a life of purpose, accomplishment, and limitless opportunity.

Debriefing

Part IV of *Be Still, Say Less* centers around empowered presence, focusing on building deeper awareness through resilience and connection. It shifts from personal transformation (Part III) to embodying that transformation and engaging with the world from a place of strength, authenticity, and interconnectedness. This section emphasizes the practical application of inner-work in navigating life's challenges and fostering meaningful relationships.

KEY THEMES

- **The Resilience Path:** This pillar explores resilience as a cultivated skill, not just an innate trait. It highlights that resilience involves adapting positively to stress, adversity, and trauma, leading to personal growth and learning. It discusses the role of family, psychological mechanisms such as cognitive reframing and emotional regulation, and the concept of post-traumatic growth.

- **Gratitude and Appreciation:** Gratitude is presented as more than just a polite gesture. It's a way of seeing and being. It's about heightened awareness, recognizing the web of support and kindness, and being present in the moment. The section emphasizes the power of acknowledgment, how gratitude fosters connection, and how it shifts focus from what's lacking to what is abundant.
- **Unlocking Potential Through Trust and Guidance:** Mentorship is highlighted as a valuable tool for self-awareness and growth. It's about receiving honest feedback, gaining perspective, and trusting the guidance of someone who has been down a similar path. It also emphasizes the importance of the mentor wanting the mentee to succeed and the reciprocal nature of mentorship.
- **Harnessing the Power of Connection:** Networking is presented as more than just a business strategy. It's about building genuine relationships. It encourages being open to new opportunities, being authentic, and planting seeds for future growth. The section emphasizes the importance of being ready, creating mutual benefit, and using networking to expand one's community and understanding.
- **Branding and Networking: Catalysts for Progress:** This pillar suggests that a strong brand opens doors, but authentic connections create lasting opportunities. It implies that personal branding should be aligned with genuine values and that networking should be about fostering meaningful relationships rather than just transactional exchanges.

Part IV is about embodying the innerwork done in previous parts and actively living from a place of empowered presence. It's about:

- **Cultivating Resilience** as a proactive approach to navigating challenges and fostering growth.
- **Practicing Gratitude** as a daily practice that enhances awareness and connection.
- **Leveraging Mentorship** for guidance, perspective, and growth.
- **Building Authentic Connections** through genuine networking and relationship building.
- **Integrating Personal Brand and Networking** to create lasting opportunities and impact.

In essence, Part IV is a guide to living a life of purpose, strength, and meaningful connection. It emphasizes that by cultivating resilience and engaging authentically with others, we can create a life of empowered presence and lasting impact.

AFFIRMATION

I embody an empowered presence through resilience, gratitude, and authentic connections. I trust guidance, build meaningful relationships, and use my unique brand to create lasting progress and impact.

SELF-REFLECTION

Part IV of *Be Still, Say Less* focuses on embodying inner-work and engaging with the world from a place of strength and authenticity. It emphasizes resilience, gratitude, mentorship, and genuine connection. Take some time to reflect on the following questions to deepen your understanding and application of these themes.

1. The Resilience Path:
- How do I currently respond to stress, adversity, and trauma? Do I see myself as a resilient person?
- What past challenges have I overcome? What strengths did I discover in myself during those times?
- How do my family dynamics influence my resilience? What coping behaviors did I learn from them?
- Do I practice cognitive reframing (changing my perspective) when facing difficulties? How can I improve my emotional regulation?
- Have I experienced post-traumatic growth where I've grown stronger or wiser after a challenging experience? Can I identify specific instances?
- What steps can I take to cultivate greater resilience in my daily life?

2. Gratitude and Appreciation:
- Do I practice gratitude regularly? How do I express it?
- Am I aware of the support and kindness that surrounds me? Do I acknowledge it?
- How present am I in the moment? Do I often dwell on the past or worry about the future?
- Do I tend to focus on what's lacking or what I'm grateful for? How can I shift my focus toward abundance?
- How does practicing gratitude affect my relationships and overall outlook on life?
- What are three things I am truly grateful for right now?

3. Unlocking Potential Through Trust and Guidance (Mentorship):

- Do I have mentors in my life? Who are they and what do they offer me?
- Am I open to receiving honest feedback and guidance from others?
- Do I trust the wisdom and experience of those who have walked a similar path?
- Am I willing to be vulnerable and ask for help when I need it?
- Do I see mentoring as a reciprocal relationship? Am I also willing to be a mentor to someone else?
- Who could I seek out as a potential mentor, and what specific guidance am I seeking?

4. Harnessing the Power of Connection (Networking):

- How do I approach networking? Do I see it as transactional or relationship-building?
- Am I open to new opportunities and perspectives when I connect with others?
- Do I strive to be authentic in my interactions?
- Am I planting seeds for future growth and collaboration?
- Do I create mutual benefit in my relationships?
- How can I expand my community and deepen my understanding through networking?

5. Branding and Networking: Catalysts for Progress:

- Does my personal brand reflect my genuine values and authenticity?

- Is my networking strategy aligned with my personal brand and goals?
- Do I prioritize building meaningful relationships over just collecting contacts?
- How can I use my brand and networking to create lasting opportunities and impact?
- Am I comfortable sharing my story and expertise with others?
- How can I ensure that my online and offline presence aligns with my true self?

6. Collaboration:
- How do I approach collaboration in my work and personal life?
- Do I value diverse perspectives and collective thinking?
- Am I creating an environment of respect, trust, and open communication in my collaborations?
- Do I prioritize shared success and fulfillment over individual achievement?
- How can I be a better collaborator and contribute to a more imaginative and transformative environment?

7. Clarity through Communication:
- Do I communicate to influence or to seek clarity?
- Am I an active listener? Do I truly understand others' perspectives?
- How can I improve my communication skills to foster genuine connection?
- Am I mindful of my nonverbal cues and body language?
- Do I create a safe space for open and honest dialogue in my relationships?

Overall Reflection:
- How well am I embodying empowered presence in my life?
- What areas of resilience and connection need the most attention and development?
- What specific action steps will I take to cultivate greater awareness and engagement?
- How can I integrate these principles into my daily interactions and decision-making?
- What does living authentically and empowered mean to me, and how will I manifest it?

By reflecting on these questions, you can gain deeper insights into your current state and identify areas for growth in building resilience and connection, leading to a more empowered presence in your life. Remember to be honest, compassionate, and open to new possibilities during this reflection process.

Part V

Mastering Stillness: Leadership, Growth, and Adaptability in a Chaotic World

P ART V IS ABOUT COMING HOME—NOT TO A PLACE, BUT to a deeper understanding of who you are. After the journey through awareness, connection, purpose, and legacy, this final section is an invitation to integrate everything you've learned and return to yourself with greater clarity, compassion, and truth. It's a reminder that wholeness is not something we chase but rather something we uncover, layer by layer, as we release what no longer serves us and reclaim what's always been within. Coming full circle means embracing the journey, honoring your growth, and standing in the fullness of your story with peace and power.

1

Cultivating Self-Leadership in a Changing World

> *True leadership begins not with the power to influence others, but with the courage to lead oneself through the ever-changing landscape of life.*
> Dr. Thurman E. Webb, Jr.

THE 21ST CENTURY IS A TIME OF UNPRECEDENTED personal and societal transformation. These shifts have profoundly affected how we connect with one another, how we align ourselves with our values and goals, and the standards we set for ourselves and others. Leadership, once reserved for a privileged few, is now recognized as a trait everyone can embody regardless of background or position. In a world where change is constant, effective leadership has moved away from rigid, prescriptive models. Instead, it's about deep self-awareness and the ability to adapt our unique strengths to the ever-changing challenges we face.

While traditional leadership research often revolves around

established theories and expert opinions, it tends to overlook the profound insights from diverse voices—especially those of African descent. Leadership, however, transcends race, profession, or social rank. It's not about titles or accolades but rather the conscious choice to take responsibility for one's actions and inspire others through personal example. Consider leaders such as Marvin Ellison, Roz Brewer, and Kenneth Frazier who rose to the helm of Fortune 500 companies not solely because of their professional competence but because they demonstrated personal leadership. Their leadership was rooted in self-awareness and resilience, values that enabled them to rise above societal expectations while staying grounded in their own identity.

Leadership, at its core, is not about a single individual steering the ship. It is about everyone standing firm in their own experiences, skills, and capabilities. Whether in business, community, or personal life, those who lead themselves well create a ripple effect of empowerment. By cultivating a sense of responsibility and purpose within, we not only contribute to the success of the organizations we are part of but foster personal growth and achievement. This self-led empowerment is critical in today's world where external circumstances are often beyond our control, yet internal leadership remains the most powerful tool at our disposal.

Marginalized individuals, in particular, demonstrate this internal leadership in profound ways. Their ability to achieve personal milestones, build thriving businesses, and attain political success is not simply due to external resources or opportunities. Rather, it stems from self-discipline, intrinsic motivation, and an unwavering dedication to personal growth. Many of these individuals face significant adversity yet succeed because they understand that true leadership begins within. Their external accomplishments are a reflection of their internal resolve, proving that leadership is first and foremost a personal journey.

Historically, marginalized groups have consistently worked to maintain a strong sense of identity in the face of external challenges. Their focus on improving not only their own lives but also the lives of those around them was both a communal and deeply personal effort. They demonstrated personal leadership by adhering to their moral and ethical standards, even when faced with systemic obstacles. This internal integrity—what we might call the "cultural beat"—became the foundation upon which they built their lives and uplifted their communities. It is a testament to the power of leading oneself first and foremost, regardless of external circumstances.

Throughout history, the social dynamics of human interaction have often been shaped by those who lead by example: Elders, spiritual figures, and everyday community members who embodied personal responsibility and moral integrity. These individuals did not necessarily hold positions of formal power, but they shaped the social fabric by living with intention and purpose. They became models for others to follow.

In exploring leadership within marginalized communities, we uncover leadership paradigms that are not always recognized in mainstream discourse. Leadership is often assumed to be the product of formal education or structured training, but much of what we know about leadership comes from the lived experiences of those who have led themselves through adversity. These individuals have forged a path through their challenges, gaining wisdom that cannot be found in textbooks or classrooms. Their leadership is a testament to the power of personal awareness, resilience, and the determination to overcome.

The process of developing leadership is consequently not a

one-size-fits-all approach. True leadership is cultivated through personal awareness and the ability to navigate one's own life with intention. It's not about waiting for someone else to show you the way but rather developing the internal clarity and strength to create your own path. Leadership is more than managing or guiding others. It's about leading yourself. When you do this effectively, you naturally inspire those around you to rise to their potential.

This kind of leadership is deeply personal. It requires a commitment to understanding oneself, one's values, and one's purpose. It involves constantly refining the ability to make conscious choices that align with who we are at our core. When we lead ourselves well, we are not only enhancing our lives but also creating a ripple effect of leadership that empowers others to do the same.

In an era where personal leadership is more critical than ever, the most powerful transformation begins with self-awareness. When we cultivate this awareness and lead from within, we unlock our full potential and create lasting change for ourselves and those around us. Leading self is not just a strategy for success. It is the foundation upon which meaningful, sustainable leadership is built.

2

The Art of Letting Go: Embracing Self-Awareness, Delegation, and Empowered Leadership

> *Leadership is knowing when to let go, trusting yourself to delegate and others to rise.*
> Dr. Thurman E. Webb, Jr.

D ELEGATION IS OFTEN VIEWED AS AN ESSENTIAL SKILL for leadership, but its true value extends beyond simply assigning tasks. It's a powerful tool for personal growth and self-leadership because delegation is not just about managing others. It involves cultivating a deep awareness of your strengths and limitations, understanding when to seek help, and knowing how to share responsibility. This shift in perspective transforms delegation from a management skill into a practice of self-awareness, allowing individuals to make intentional decisions about how they manage their time, energy, and resources.

One of the most empowering aspects of delegation is the realization that you don't have to do everything yourself. Many people fall into the trap of believing that handling every task personally is the only way to ensure it's done right. This mindset can lead to burnout and diminished performance. By delegating, you give yourself permission to focus on what truly matters such as tasks that align with your strengths and long-term goals. For example, if you're an entrepreneur with a clear strategic vision but struggle with administrative tasks, it's more effective to delegate bookkeeping, scheduling, or data entry. Doing so not only lightens your load but also frees your mental energy to focus on growth, innovation, and the areas where you can have the most impact.

Delegation also requires a deep understanding of your own abilities. Knowing when and what to delegate means recognizing where your time and effort are best spent. This type of self-awareness comes through reflection and honest self-assessment. Ask yourself: What tasks drain my energy? What responsibilities am I consistently avoiding or rushing through? Once you identify these areas, you can make informed decisions about which tasks to delegate, ensuring that your energy is conserved for the work that plays to your strengths and fuels your passion.

Consider the example of a student juggling academics, part-time work, and personal responsibilities. Many students feel overwhelmed by the need to excel in all areas, leading to stress and exhaustion. But through self-awareness, a student can recognize that they cannot do everything at once. Instead of trying to tackle everything solo, they can delegate by forming study groups with each member specializing in a different area of the course. This not only lightens their individual workload but also creates a collaborative environment where everyone benefits from shared strengths. In this way, delegation becomes a tool for working smarter not harder, fostering mutual support and shared success.

In personal life, delegation is just as important. Many people feel overwhelmed by daily responsibilities, whether it's managing a household, caring for loved ones, or juggling financial duties. By delegating tasks within the household such as assigning chores to children or sharing responsibilities with a partner, stress can be significantly reduced and a sense of balance restored. For example, a parent balancing a demanding job and family responsibilities might find relief in assigning specific chores to each family member. Not only does this lighten the parent's load, but it also empowers others by teaching responsibility and teamwork. In this context, delegation isn't just about reducing your workload. It's about fostering independence and competence in others, creating a shared sense of ownership and collaboration.

Delegation, at its heart, is also a practice of trust. When you delegate, you're not just offloading tasks but rather entrusting others with responsibility. This trust strengthens relationships, builds collaboration, and often results in better outcomes. Delegation also hones your own leadership and communication skills. For instance, if you're managing a project and delegate specific responsibilities to team members, you need to communicate expectations clearly and offer guidance. This forces you to reflect on your needs, articulate your vision, and become more deliberate in your actions and decisions. Each skill is essential to effective self-leadership.

Delegation also nurtures a growth mindset. By trusting others to take on tasks, you create opportunities for learning and development for yourself and for those to whom you delegate. In a work setting, this can be transformative. A manager who delegates critical responsibilities to team members allows them to step up, learn new skills, and take on greater accountability. Simultaneously, the manager sharpens their mentoring and leadership abilities, creating a cycle of growth that benefits everyone. This growth-oriented approach fosters an environment where success is a shared journey versus an individual accomplishment.

Throughout these examples, one truth remains: Effective delegation begins with self-awareness. Understanding your strengths and limitations enables you to delegate with purpose and intention. It's the recognition that you don't have to bear the weight of everything on your shoulders. By consciously sharing responsibility, you instead create space for your growth while empowering others to step into their own potential.

When viewed through the lens of self-awareness, delegation becomes an act of personal empowerment. It allows you to manage your life in a way that's sustainable, efficient, and focused on what truly matters. It's a form of self-care, protecting your energy and enabling you to focus on your core strengths. More than that, it's an act of leadership for yourself and others. Delegation fosters growth, builds trust, and creates a ripple effect of leadership by example.

Delegation goes beyond being just a productivity tactic. It's a reflection of mindful leadership. It requires self-awareness to identify where your strengths can make the most impact and the confidence to entrust others to excel in areas where they can thrive. Delegating with purpose creates opportunities for your own success and the success of those around you. By embodying intentional leadership, you lead not only through action but by demonstrating how to live with purpose, clarity, and the wisdom to know when to share the responsibility.

3

Transforming Conflict: Leading Through Creative Abrasion

Conflict, when embraced with self-awareness and empathy, becomes a doorway to deeper understanding and empowered relationships.
Dr. Thurman E. Webb, Jr.

CONFLICT IS AN INHERENT PART OF ANY HUMAN INTERACTION, particularly in corporate and academic environments where emotions, power dynamics, and personal investments run high. In the corporate world, conflicts often stem from power struggles, ego satisfaction, dependency, and issues of credibility. These factors can intensify disputes, leading to poor agreements or prolonged stalemates. When conflict remains unresolved, it can lead to covert actions and undermine the effectiveness of an organization. Resolving conflicts amicably and fostering a win-win mindset is not only in the best interest of the organization but also essential for individual growth and leadership development.

But what is conflict, really? At its core, conflict arises when individuals or groups perceive that the actions, behaviors, or intentions of others do not align with their own values or expectations. It is a situation that calls for action to bring these differing values closer together. In an organizational context, conflict often arises from behavior issues, poor communication, unclear roles, breaches of trust, and resistance to change. These are all factors to consider when developing effective strategies for navigating diversity and inclusion in the workplace.

Historically Black Colleges and Universities (HBCUs) and other minority-serving institutions are examples of environments where individuals from diverse backgrounds come together. In these spaces, conflict can arise as students and faculty learn to navigate different values, beliefs, and behaviors. These environments also provide fertile ground for learning how to address conflicts related to race, culture, and identity, thus fostering growth and understanding.

Reflecting on my own experience, I learned about conflict resolution firsthand during my time as an undergraduate student at Tennessee State University. One particular incident stands out. A group project spiraled into chaos due to a heated disagreement between two classmates whom I'll call Shark and Turtle. What began as a simple discussion about project topics escalated into a standoff, with each refusing to budge. With only a day left before the presentation deadline, the tension in the room was palpable. We had made little progress, and I felt like I was in the middle of a Mexican standoff with all guns drawn, pointed at each other, and no way to win.

Sensing the urgency of the situation, I decided to take action even though I wasn't the group leader. I suggested we take a break and continue the conversation over lunch, specifically pizza that was my treat. Over a shared meal, I started the conversation by acknowledging the underlying issues. Turtle felt his ideas were being dismissed, while Shark believed Turtle wasn't seeing the bigger picture of the project's requirements. Rather than focusing on who was right or wrong, I guided the conversation toward understanding their deeper concerns and motivations.

Through active listening and empathy, we were able to uncover that both Shark and Turtle had the same goal: To earn a good grade and complete the project on time. By acknowledging each other's perspectives and finding common ground, we were able to settle on a solution that worked for everyone. We created a shared template with a less in-depth dive into the project topic. The conflict was resolved not by brute force or dominance but through collaboration and understanding. In that moment, I witnessed the power of empathy and effective communication in transforming conflict into a renewed sense of teamwork.

This experience taught me that people approach conflict differently based on their personality and experiences. Some like Shark tackle conflict head-on, using direct confrontation to address issues. Others like Turtle avoid conflict altogether, preferring to withdraw rather than engage. Both approaches have their strengths and weaknesses. Sharks are unafraid to engage in tough conversations, keeping people in line and addressing issues directly. They can, however, sometimes be overly aggressive and push others away. Turtles, on the other hand, avoid conflict to protect themselves but in doing so, they miss opportunities to develop their conflict resolution skills.

Just as individuals have different approaches to conflict, organizations and leaders must recognize that conflict can be resolved in multiple ways. The most effective method is the collaborative approach, which seeks a "win-win" outcome for both parties.

Collaboration focuses on understanding the needs and goals of each party involved and finding a solution that benefits everyone. This approach deepens understanding, strengthens relationships, and fosters a sense of shared purpose.

In a collaborative conflict resolution, questions such as "What can we do that benefits both of us?" or "How can we solve this problem together?" open the door to dialogue and mutual understanding. The goal is not to win or dominate but to reach a solution that leaves both parties feeling heard and respected. In doing so, the relationship between the parties grows stronger, creating a foundation for future cooperation.

Successful conflict resolution also requires the development of key skills, particularly the ability to foster open dialogue. These skills are best learned through real-life experiences and examples where leaders model the behaviors they wish to instill in others. Whether in the classroom, workplace, or community, conflict resolution is most effective when leaders demonstrate empathy, active listening, and the ability to navigate disagreements constructively.

At the heart of conflict resolution is the belief that something positive can emerge from the process. When handled effectively, conflict can strengthen relationships, increase mutual understanding, and create a shared sense of purpose. Whether the outcome is a complete resolution or a decision to manage ongoing differences, the goal of conflict resolution should always be to preserve and improve relationships. The process should foster an environment where future interactions are built on trust, respect, and collaboration.

In both personal and professional settings, conflict is inevitable. With awareness and the right approach, however, conflict can be transformed into an opportunity for growth as individuals and within an organization. By stepping into leadership with self-awareness and empathy, we can influence others and create an environment where collaboration, understanding, and mutual respect thrive. In this way, conflict is no longer a barrier but a bridge to deeper connection and shared success.

4

Harnessing Emotional Intelligence for Personal Growth and Fulfillment

> *Emotional intelligence is the gateway to deeper self-awareness, guiding us to navigate life's challenges with empathy, resilience, and clarity.*
> Dr. Thurman E. Webb, Jr.

EMOTIONAL INTELLIGENCE IS MORE THAN A CORPORATE buzzword. It's a foundational life skill that plays a crucial role in personal well-being and influences how we interact with the world. At its core, emotional intelligence refers to the ability to recognize, understand, and manage your own emotions while also being attuned to the emotions of others. This skill allows individuals to navigate life's challenges with greater ease and clarity, resulting in healthier relationships, better decision-making, and a more balanced approach to personal growth.

Daniel Goleman, a pioneer in the field of emotional intelligence, outlined five key components that form its backbone: Self-awareness, self-regulation, motivation, empathy, and social skills. These elements are essential for professional success and also play a vital role in personal development and emotional health. When applied to everyday life, emotional intelligence becomes a powerful tool for enhancing emotional and psychological well-being, leading to greater life satisfaction.

The cornerstone of emotional intelligence is self-awareness—the ability to recognize and understand your own emotions and how they influence your thoughts and actions. Imagine a scenario where you're feeling frustrated or angry. Without self-awareness, you might react impulsively and say or do something you later regret. By being aware of your emotional state, you can stop, reflect, and identify the root cause of your frustration. This pause allows for thoughtful action rather than reactive behavior, fostering emotional resilience and contributing to mental well-being. In personal relationships, self-awareness helps prevent unnecessary arguments as it allows you to assess whether your emotional response is proportionate to the situation.

Building on self-awareness is self-regulation, the ability to manage your emotions in a constructive manner. It's about maintaining control, especially in emotionally charged situations, and responding thoughtfully instead of reacting on instinct. For example, when you're under stress or in the midst of conflict, self-regulation helps you keep your emotions in check, ensuring that you respond calmly rather than lashing out. This skill is critical for maintaining healthy relationships as well as managing stress and anxiety. People with high emotional intelligence often practice mindfulness, deep breathing, or journaling as ways to process emotions and prevent them from becoming overwhelming.

Motivation is another key component of emotional intelligence and refers to the internal drive to pursue goals despite obstacles. This intrinsic motivation does not come from external rewards but rather a deep sense of purpose and fulfillment. When working toward a personal goal–whether completing a degree, training for a marathon, or improving relationships–setbacks are inevitable. Emotional intelligence helps you stay focused on the bigger picture, recognizing that challenges are part of the process. This internal drive keeps you resilient even when circumstances become difficult and allows you to persevere to ultimately succeed.

Empathy, the ability to understand and share the feelings of others, is the foundation of emotional intelligence in personal relationships. Empathy allows you to connect with others on a deeper level, fostering trust and understanding. For instance, when a friend is going through a tough time, empathy enables you to put yourself in their shoes and offer genuine support. Practicing empathy strengthens relationships and improves your ability to navigate social situations with greater sensitivity, reducing conflicts and encouraging collaboration.

Finally, social skills encompass the ability to manage relationships effectively and navigate social interactions with ease. You don't need to be highly extroverted to develop strong social skills but rather clearly understand the dynamics of relationships and communicating. These skills are essential for resolving conflicts, setting boundaries, and building connections. Whether expressing your needs in a relationship or collaborating on a project, strong social skills contribute to both personal and interpersonal success.

A real-life example of emotional intelligence in action can be seen in how we handle conflict. Imagine you're in a disagreement with a close friend or family member. Without emotional intelligence, this conflict might escalate, leading to hurt feelings and broken communication. Emotional intelligence allows you to approach the situation differently. Self-awareness helps you recognize your emotional triggers, self-regulation keeps you calm, empathy allows you to understand the other person's perspective, and social skills enable you to communicate effectively. As a result, the conflict is more likely to be resolved in a way that strengthens the relationship rather than damaging it.

Cultural awareness also plays a significant role in emotional intelligence, particularly for individuals from marginalized communities. People of color, for instance, often navigate environments that expose them to microaggressions or biases. Emotional intelligence is invaluable in these situations, helping individuals recognize the emotional toll of these experiences while equipping them with tools to respond constructively. For example, when faced with a microaggression, emotional intelligence helps you manage your immediate emotional response while also understanding the broader social dynamics at play. Over time, this skill can help create more inclusive and respectful environments through constructive dialogue.

Oprah Winfrey is a powerful public figure who exemplifies emotional intelligence. Despite facing significant personal challenges, Oprah has consistently used her platform to connect with diverse audiences through empathy, self-awareness, and effective communication. Her ability to create meaningful conversations in public and behind the scenes is a testament to emotional intelligence's transformative power. Oprah's story demonstrates that it isn't just a tool for professional success but rather a key to personal fulfillment, allowing individuals to navigate life with purpose and resilience.

Emotional intelligence is an essential skill for leading a balanced and fulfilling life. By nurturing self-awareness, self-regulation, motivation, empathy, and social skills, you enhance your emotional well-being and foster stronger relationships to create a more purposeful existence. Emotional intelligence equips you to navigate life's highs and lows with clarity, fostering deeper connections with others and a more grounded sense of self. At its core, developing emotional intelligence is about expanding your awareness of yourself and the world around you.

5

Growing Through Change: The Power of Adaptability

Adaptability is the wisdom to grow through change, turning uncertainty into opportunity and obstacles into pathways.
Dr. Thurman E. Webb, Jr.

ADAPTABILITY IS A CORNERSTONE OF SUCCESS PERSONALLY and professionally. It's the ability to embrace change, adjust our mindset, and navigate uncertainty with resilience and grace. As Maya Angelou once said, "If you don't like something, change it. If you can't change it, change your attitude." This powerful message captures the essence of adaptability, the understanding that while we may not always have control over our circumstances, we can always control how we respond to them. In a world that is ever evolving, adaptability is no longer a luxury but rather a necessity. It is the key to unlocking growth, turning challenges into opportunities, and flourishing in an environment that often feels unpredictable.

At its core, adaptability is not just about reacting to change but anticipating it, embracing it, and using it as a tool for progress. It involves a wide range of skills from self-awareness and emotional intelligence to lifelong learning and effective communication. Being adaptable means remaining open to new ideas and being ready to pivot when necessary while remaining resilient in the face of obstacles. In today's fast-paced, interconnected world, those who can adapt are better positioned to thrive. Adaptability allows individuals to not only survive change but use it as a stepping stone to success.

One of the key pillars of adaptability is the willingness to continuously learn. Lifelong learning is essential in an era where industries, technologies, and even societal norms are constantly evolving. This doesn't mean just formal education but rather staying curious, seeking out new information, and being open to experiences that push us out of our comfort zones. In a rapidly changing job market, those who make learning a priority are better equipped to handle the unexpected. This attitude of growth helps people remain relevant, ensuring that they can adapt to new roles, technologies, and challenges as they arise.

Self-awareness is another critical component of adaptability. Knowing our strengths, weaknesses, and emotional responses allows us to adjust to change more effectively. When we are in tune with ourselves, we can better assess how different situations impact us and what actions are necessary to navigate them. Self-awareness helps us recognize when it's time to shift our approach, pivot our goals, or rethink our strategies. It's the foundation of emotional resilience, the ability to stay grounded and flexible even when life doesn't go as planned. Adaptability requires introspection as it often involves letting go of old habits, mindsets, or ways of doing things that may no longer serve us well.

In professional settings, adaptability is often what separates leaders from followers. The modern workplace is constantly evolving, and the ability to adapt to new technologies, changing team dynamics, and shifting market demands is crucial for success. Whether it's learning a new skill, navigating a career transition, or leading a team through a period of uncertainty, adaptability empowers professionals to remain flexible and proactive. It enables them to see challenges as opportunities for innovation and growth rather than as roadblocks. In this way, adaptability becomes a mindset versus a skill and a way of approaching the world with curiosity, openness, and resilience.

Adaptability isn't just about personal growth but rather collective progress. In any organization or community, adaptability is what drives innovation and fosters a culture of inclusion. To truly thrive, companies must create environments where adaptability is encouraged and valued. This means fostering a workplace culture that embraces diversity, welcomes different perspectives, and encourages individuals to take risks and think creatively. When organizations value adaptability, they create space for growth, not just for individuals but for the entire organization.

Diversity plays a key role in adaptability, particularly in professional settings. Diverse teams bring together a wide range of perspectives, experiences, and ideas, which are crucial for solving complex problems and fostering innovation. For diversity to truly thrive, however, adaptability must be present. People must be willing to learn from one another, to embrace different ways of thinking, and to adapt their approaches based on the strengths of their team members. In this sense, adaptability is the bridge between diversity and inclusion. It allows organizations to leverage the full potential of their teams by fostering an environment where everyone's contributions are valued.

Historically, the ability to adapt has been especially critical for those who have faced systemic barriers, particularly African Americans. For centuries, adaptability has been a survival skill, enabling individuals and communities to navigate systems and environments that were not designed for their success. From the long fight for civil rights to the ongoing struggle for racial equity, African Americans have had to be adaptable in order to overcome institutionalized obstacles. This adaptability and resilience in the face of adversity has been a defining feature of the African American experience and offers lessons for everyone about the power of perseverance and flexibility.

Adaptability is not only about responding to external challenges but also about internal growth. As individuals, we are constantly evolving. Our ability to adapt to personal changes is just as important as adapting to the world around us. Our values, goals, and aspirations shift as we move through different stages of life. Personal adaptability means being open to re-evaluating our paths, changing our minds, and allowing ourselves the flexibility to grow in unexpected ways. It's about recognizing that change is not something to fear but rather embrace as part of the journey.

One of the greatest challenges we face in life is uncertainty. We can never fully predict what the future will hold, whether in our careers, relationships, or society at large. This is where adaptability becomes a truly invaluable asset. When we cultivate adaptability, we equip ourselves with the tools to face uncertainty with confidence. Rather than fearing the unknown, we learn to welcome it, seeing it as an opportunity for growth and transformation. Adaptability teaches us that while we may not be able to control everything, we can always control how we respond.

In professional environments, adaptability is often the determining factor in career success. In a world where industries are constantly evolving and technological advancements are reshaping the workforce, those who can adapt to change are the ones who thrive. Whether it's learning new skills, transitioning to a new role, or leading a team through a period of upheaval, adaptability is essential for staying relevant and competitive. Leaders who can adapt are able to guide their teams through uncertainty, find creative solutions to problems, and seize new opportunities as they arise.

Of course, adaptability isn't without its challenges. It requires a level of vulnerability and openness to change that can feel uncomfortable or even threatening. Adapting to new circumstances often means letting go of old habits, mindsets, or ways of doing things that have become familiar. It requires us to confront our fears, step outside of our comfort zones, and embrace the unknown. But it is precisely this willingness to be vulnerable that makes adaptability such a powerful tool for growth.

At its heart, adaptability is about resilience. It's the ability to bounce back from setbacks, learn from failure, and keep moving forward. Whether in personal relationships, career development, or navigating societal changes, resilience allows us to stay focused on our goals, even in the face of adversity. Adaptability and resilience go hand in hand as both require an attitude of perseverance and an unwavering belief in our ability to succeed despite challenges.

In today's rapidly changing world, adaptability is more than just a skill. It's a mindset that empowers individuals to thrive. It allows us to remain open to new possibilities, to embrace diversity in thought and experience, and to continuously learn and grow. Whether we are adapting to technological advancements, career transitions, or personal changes, adaptability is the key to navigating life's uncertainties with confidence and grace.

Adaptability empowers us to turn challenges into opportunities. It serves as the cornerstone for building resilience, fostering growth, and achieving success. In an ever-changing world, developing adaptability is crucial not just for survival but for thriving. It enables us to evolve in ways that allow us to live with purpose and fulfillment, embracing the uncertainties of life as opportunities for growth and transformation.

6

Unlocking Potential with a Growth Mindset

> *Growth begins where comfort ends. It is in the challenges we face and the effort we give that we unlock our true potential.*
> Dr. Thurman E. Webb, Jr.

THE CONCEPT OF A GROWTH MINDSET HAS RESHAPED our understanding of how we approach challenges, learning, and success. Introduced by Stanford University psychologist Carol Dweck, growth mindset is built on the belief that abilities, intelligence, and talents are not fixed traits but can be developed over time through effort, dedication, and perseverance. This mindset fosters a perspective that embraces challenges as opportunities for growth, sees mistakes as valuable lessons, and views hard work as the path to success. In an ever-changing world, adopting a growth mindset is essential for personal and professional development.

THE FOUNDATION OF A GROWTH MINDSET

At the heart of a growth mindset is the understanding that abilities are malleable and can be nurtured through consistent effort and learning. The brain, much like a muscle, strengthens and grows when challenged. Those with a growth mindset recognize that their potential is not determined by innate talent but by their willingness to put in the effort to improve. This belief fosters resilience, encouraging individuals to face obstacles with the confidence that they can grow and adapt.

This mindset allows individuals to approach challenges with a sense of curiosity and optimism, understanding that every new experience provides an opportunity to stretch their capabilities. Whether in education, work, or personal endeavors, a growth mindset drives continuous improvement and encourages individuals to take risks and step beyond their comfort zones.

EMBRACING CHALLENGES AND LEARNING FROM MISTAKES

One of the defining qualities of a growth mindset is the way individuals respond to challenges. Instead of avoiding difficult tasks, those with a growth mindset seek them out, knowing that growth occurs in the face of adversity. Challenges are not viewed as barriers but necessary steps in the process of learning and self-improvement. This mindset encourages people to see difficult situations as chances to push their limits and expand their knowledge.

Mistakes are another critical aspect of the growth mindset. Rather than fearing failure, individuals with a growth mindset understand that mistakes are an inevitable and valuable part of the learning process. Every mistake is seen as a learning opportunity—an invitation to reflect, adjust, and try again. This perspective helps individuals build resilience, enabling them to bounce back from setbacks and keep moving forward with greater determination.

LIFELONG LEARNING AND CONTINUOUS IMPROVEMENT

A core principle of the growth mindset is the commitment to lifelong learning. Those who adopt this mindset are always eager to expand their knowledge and skills, knowing that growth doesn't stop with formal education. They actively seek out new experiences, read widely, and pursue new challenges, understanding that continuous learning is key to staying adaptable in an ever-evolving world.

In professional settings, this commitment to learning is a significant advantage. As industries and technologies change, those with a growth mindset are better equipped to adapt and stay relevant. They don't shy away from learning new skills or taking on projects outside their comfort zones because they see every opportunity as a chance to grow.

This attitude toward learning isn't limited to professional skills but rather extends to personal growth as well. Individuals with a growth mindset apply the same principles to their relationships, hobbies, and self-care as they constantly seek ways to improve and enrich their lives. This ongoing pursuit of knowledge keeps them flexible, open-minded, and better able to navigate change.

GROWTH MINDSET AND PROFESSIONAL SUCCESS

In the workplace, a growth mindset can be a game-changer. Individuals who believe in their capacity to grow are more likely to seek out professional development opportunities, take on leadership roles, and innovate within their teams. They are willing to tackle difficult problems, experiment with new ideas, and invest time and effort into their own growth and the success of their organization.

Organizations that foster a culture of growth mindset benefit from employees who are engaged, resilient, and committed to continuous improvement. These employees are not afraid to take calculated risks or challenge the status quo because they understand that true innovation often comes from trial and error. They view setbacks as part of the process, allowing them to remain motivated and solution-focused in the face of adversity.

Leaders with a growth mindset are particularly effective in creating dynamic, forward-thinking teams. By modeling a commitment to learning and embracing challenges, these leaders inspire their teams to adopt the same mindset. This fosters a collaborative environment where team members feel empowered to contribute ideas, take on new challenges, and grow both individually and collectively.

CULTIVATING A GROWTH MINDSET

While some people may naturally lean toward a growth mindset, it is a perspective that can be cultivated with intentional effort. Developing a growth mindset begins with recognizing how we approach challenges and setbacks. Do we view them as insurmountable obstacles, or do we see them as opportunities to learn and grow? By shifting our perspective and embracing the idea that effort leads to improvement, we can begin to rewire our thinking.

One way to cultivate a growth mindset is to focus on the process rather than the outcome. Individuals with a growth mindset value the effort and learning that comes with pursuing a goal rather than being solely concerned with immediate success. This shift in focus encourages persistence, as individuals are motivated by the progress they make along the way rather than being discouraged by temporary setbacks.

Another key strategy is to actively seek out feedback. Those with a growth mindset view feedback as valuable information that can help them improve versus criticism. By embracing constructive feedback and using it to guide their development, individuals can accelerate their growth and make meaningful progress toward their goals.

Finally, surrounding oneself with a supportive community is essential to cultivating a growth mindset. When individuals are connected with others who value learning, resilience, and effort, they are more likely to adopt those same attitudes. Whether in the workplace, in educational settings, or in personal relationships, being part of a culture that encourages growth reinforces the belief that effort and perseverance lead to success.

THE BENEFITS OF A GROWTH MINDSET

The benefits of a growth mindset are far-reaching. In education, students with a growth mindset are more motivated to learn, take on challenging tasks, and persist through difficulties. They understand that intelligence is not fixed and that with effort, they can improve their abilities. This leads to higher academic achievement and greater engagement in learning.

In professional environments, a growth mindset drives innovation and leadership. Individuals who believe in their capacity to grow are more willing to take risks, pursue ambitious goals, and lead teams through uncertainty. This mindset fosters resilience, enabling professionals to adapt to change and thrive in challenging environments.

Perhaps most importantly, a growth mindset cultivates resilience and well-being. By embracing challenges, learning from mistakes, and committing to lifelong growth, individuals with a growth mindset are better equipped to handle life's inevitable ups and downs. They approach difficulties with confidence, knowing that they have the ability to learn and improve with time and effort.

A growth mindset is more than just a belief. It is a way of approaching life that empowers individuals to unlock their full potential. It fosters resilience, encourages continuous learning, and enables people to turn challenges into opportunities for growth. Whether in education, the workplace, or personal life, adopting a growth mindset allows us to embrace the process of improvement, understanding that our abilities can always be developed through effort and perseverance. By cultivating this mindset, we can navigate life's uncertainties with confidence and unlock the power to grow, adapt, and succeed.

7

The Role of Risk-Taking in Personal and Professional Growth

Risk-taking can be an act of empowerment.
Dr. Thurman E. Webb, Jr.

IN THE PROFESSIONAL REALM, RISK-TAKING CAN BE compared to making investments in the financial world. Calculated risks are taken with the hope of achieving high returns. In finance, efficient markets allocate capital to the most productive uses, rewarding those willing to take on risk. Similarly, in the professional world, individuals who take career risks can also experience great rewards, though the process is less clearly understood. Unlike in finance, where risk-taking is well-accepted, career risk often carries higher personal stakes. Decisions to pursue a new path, take on a challenging role, or commit to an ambitious project require careful consideration of the potential benefits and the value of taking such a leap.

Risk-taking in a professional context is often viewed narrowly as a financial investment, but it encompasses much more. As we explore the dynamics of professional success, it's important to broaden this definition to include career commitment, innovation, and personal growth. Taking career risks is not just about seeking promotions or starting a business. It's about embracing uncertainty, pushing beyond comfort zones, and pursuing opportunities with unknown outcomes.

THE HISTORICAL CONTEXT OF RISK-TAKING IN BLACK AMERICA

Risk-taking within the Black American experience has deep roots shaped by a long history of oppression and struggle. From the enslavement of Black men, women, and children during the Trans-Atlantic slave trade to the systemic inequalities that persist today, the Black community has often faced unique and significant risks simply by asserting autonomy or pursuing economic opportunities.

This historical legacy of risk is exemplified by figures such as Nat Turner, who in 1831 led a rebellion against the institution of slavery. While Turner's actions resulted in his execution, his willingness to take a monumental risk became a catalyst for the Abolitionist Movement. His rebellion highlighted that for many Black individuals, taking risks has not just been about personal gain but challenging systemic injustice and empowering the broader community.

BLACK ENTREPRENEURSHIP AND RISK-TAKING

Entrepreneurship has long been a path through which Black Americans have taken risks to build a better future. In the years before and after the Emancipation Proclamation, Black entrepreneurs faced extraordinary dangers in pursuit of economic independence. Many risked their lives, savings, and reputations to create opportunities for themselves and their communities. Some faced violence and financial ruin while others, such as Madam C.J. Walker, found success against all odds.

Often recognized as one of the first Black female entrepreneurs, Walker built a beauty empire by creating products for Black women. Her success was not only personal but opened doors for many other Black women by providing them with employment opportunities and encouraging them to pursue financial independence. Walker's story illustrates that for Black entrepreneurs, the risks are not just financial. They also carry the weight of cultural and societal impact.

NAVIGATING SYSTEMIC BARRIERS

One of the most significant dimensions of risk-taking for Black professionals is the additional challenge of navigating systemic barriers. Racial discrimination, economic inequality, and social exclusion pose risks that go beyond those faced by others. Taking professional risks as a Black individual often means confronting the possibility of failure in environments where the stakes are higher and where one mistake can confirm damaging stereotypes or set back hard-earned progress.

This heightened risk requires a careful balance between ambition and strategy. Black professionals must weigh their decisions with an acute awareness of the societal dynamics that shape their experiences. This context adds complexity to career decisions where risks may involve not only personal outcomes but broader implications for one's community and legacy.

STRATEGIC RISK-TAKING AND MODERN SUCCESS

Despite these challenges, many Black professionals have embraced risk-taking as a strategy for success. Billionaire businessman Robert F. Smith, for example, made his mark by taking calculated risks in the tech investment space. By focusing on underserved sectors and aligning his business ventures with a commitment to social impact, Smith demonstrated how strategic risk-taking can lead to both financial success and positive societal change, something no other organization was doing at the time.

Smith shows us that risk-taking is not just about financial gain but rather empowerment. For Black professionals, taking risks can serve as a declaration of self-determination and a challenge to systemic limitations. By pursuing ambitious goals and creating spaces for others to thrive, individuals such as Smith highlight the transformative power of risk in reshaping professional and social landscapes.

RISK-TAKING AS EMPOWERMENT AND GROWTH

Ultimately, risk-taking in the professional world is not merely about the potential for success but rather empowerment. It's about asserting agency in the face of uncertainty and pursuing growth, both personally and collectively. For Black professionals, this journey involves navigating additional layers of challenge, but it also holds the potential for profound rewards. By embracing calculated risks, building strong support networks, and drawing from the rich legacy of those who have come before, individuals can move forward with confidence and resilience.

Risk-taking offers opportunities for personal development, career advancement, and communal progress. It involves stepping boldly into new ventures, knowing that challenges are part of the process. The path of risk-taking is rarely easy, but it is essential for those seeking to break barriers, create change, and pave the way for future generations.

Risk-taking is a critical component of professional success and for Black individuals, it carries a unique set of challenges and opportunities. Turner and Walker exemplify the ways in which risk has played a role in shaping not only individual success but also broader societal change. Today, professionals such as Smith continue this legacy by taking strategic risks that benefit both their careers and their communities.

WHAT IT ALL MEANS

For Black professionals, risk-taking is more than just a career strategy. It is an act of empowerment and a means of asserting control in a world that often imposes limitations. By embracing calculated risks and navigating the complexities of systemic barriers, individuals can not only achieve personal success but contribute to the growth and resilience of their communities.

The journey of risk-taking is filled with challenges, but it is also rich with opportunities for growth and transformation. As individuals step into new ventures with courage and purpose, they honor the legacy of those who have come before, empower their present, and create a path for future generations to follow.

8

Time Management: Creating Harmony and Achievement

> *Mastering time isn't about doing more. It's about aligning your moments with what truly matters, creating space for both achievement and joy.*
> Dr. Thurman E. Webb, Jr.

FOR YEARS, I STRUGGLED WITH TIME MANAGEMENT. No matter how hard I worked, it felt as if there were never enough hours in the day to keep up with everything. I juggled multiple roles at work, at home, and in my personal life. I always seemed to fall behind. Deadlines slipped, tasks piled up, and I found myself constantly playing catch-up. That was when I realized the key to managing my time more effectively wasn't just about working harder but rather working smarter. The solution? A universal calendar.

A universal calendar changed the way I approached time. Instead of keeping separate calendars for work and personal life with one for meetings and another for social events, I brought everything together into one place. By uniting all my responsibilities, appointments, and commitments into a single calendar, I gained a clear, comprehensive view of my time. I wasn't just managing work tasks or family obligations in isolation. I could see the big picture of my entire life and with that clarity came control.

This calendar wasn't just for work meetings or deadlines. It was for everything from gym sessions to family dinners and those rare moments of relaxation. Each event had a place in the schedule. This holistic view allowed me to balance my time in a way I had never been able to before. Suddenly, I wasn't just reacting to the demands of the day. I was creating a life that made space for work, personal growth, and enjoyment.

BUILDING THE UNIVERSAL CALENDAR

The first step to building my universal calendar was simple: I added everything. Every appointment, every deadline, every personal task. Nothing was left out. Whether it was a client meeting or an hour for reading, I treated all my commitments with equal importance. After all, the time I spent on myself or with my family was just as valuable as time spent working. This approach helped me see where my time was really going.

For the first time, I had a full picture of how my day would look from start to finish. There was no guessing, no fragmented to-do lists scattered across different apps or planners. With one glance, I could see everything that needed my attention at work and at home. That allowed me to prioritize more effectively. I began to notice patterns in how I used my time, where I was overcommitting, and where I could carve out moments for myself.

THE TIME LOG: TRACKING PROGRESS

Once my universal calendar was in place, I introduced a time log to track my progress. A time log works hand in hand with the calendar to ensure that I'm staying on track. It's not just about planning but rather making sure I stick to the plan. The time log showed me how I was actually using my time, revealing areas where I got distracted or wasted minutes.

For instance, I had a habit of spending too much time on minor tasks such as checking emails without realizing how much of my day it consumed. Seeing this on my time log made me more mindful of how I was allocating my hours. It helped me refine my universal calendar to reflect not only what I wanted to accomplish but also how long it realistically took to get things done. The more I tracked, the more accurate and effective my planning became.

THE NONRENEWABLE NATURE OF TIME

Time is the one resource we all share, and it's nonrenewable. Once it's spent, it's gone forever. A universal calendar helped me appreciate the importance of how I used each minute. There are 24 hours in a day, no more, no less. What I did with them was entirely up to me. I began to ask myself, "Am I spending my time or investing it?"

I realized that we have four options when it comes to time: Waste it, spend it, invest it, or enjoy it. Wasting time brought no return. Spending it could be useful but didn't always lead to growth. The true value came from investing time in things that mattered, whether that was personal development, relationships, or career goals. And of course, there was always time to enjoy life, which was just as important for maintaining balance and well-being.

With this perspective shift, I started viewing time as precious capital. Just like money, time needed to be allocated wisely. A universal calendar helped me invest my time in the things that mattered most at work and in my personal life. It wasn't about squeezing in more tasks but rather making sure the time I spent was meaningful.

TIME MANAGEMENT FOR BALANCE, NOT JUST PRODUCTIVITY

One of the most important lessons I learned through using a universal calendar was that time management isn't just about squeezing more productivity out of every day. It's about finding balance. In the past, I would focus so much on work tasks that I'd neglect my personal life. With a universal calendar, I could see how my day was divided and ensure that I was making time for everything that mattered.

I began to schedule time for things such as relaxation, exercise, and connecting with loved ones, all of which are often overlooked when we're busy trying to be "productive." The calendar wasn't just for work anymore. It was for life. I realized that managing my time effectively meant making sure I had space to recharge, reflect, and enjoy life.

THE UNIVERSAL CALENDAR: A LESSON IN SELF-LOVE

Using a universal calendar taught me a valuable lesson in self-love. I learned that respecting my time was a form of respecting myself. Making space in my schedule for things that brought me joy wasn't selfish but rather essential. Whether it was taking a break to read, spending time with friends, or simply resting, giving myself permission to enjoy life made me a better, more focused person when it came to work.

Time management, I discovered, is as much about honoring yourself as it is about achieving goals. By prioritizing time for both work and personal fulfillment, I felt more in control of my life. The universal calendar wasn't just a tool for organizing tasks. It became a reflection of my values and priorities.

TIME AS A PATH TO FULFILLMENT

A universal calendar transformed the way I manage my time, shifting my perspective from viewing life as a collection of scattered tasks to seeing it as a cohesive whole. By integrating personal and professional commitments, I found a new sense of balance and was able to prioritize what truly matters most.

Time is a finite resource but by managing it wisely, we can live richer, fuller lives. A universal calendar helps us do that by giving us a clear view of where our time is going and how we can invest it in ways that bring joy, success, and fulfillment. Time management isn't just about productivity. It's about living a life that reflects our true priorities and values.

9

The Transformative Power of Public Speaking

> *Public speaking is not just about finding your voice. It's about owning your story,*
> Dr. Thurman E. Webb, Jr.

PUBLIC SPEAKING HAS ALWAYS INTRIGUED ME. LIKE MANY people, I was once terrified of standing in front of a crowd with the spotlight shining too brightly, my nerves tightening, and my voice shaking. I was no natural-born speaker but over time, I came to understand that public speaking offers benefits far beyond what I had initially imagined. The ability to speak confidently and clearly in front of others is not just about overcoming fear. It's a vital skill that can open doors to countless opportunities.

In my early career, I began to notice a pattern: Those who excelled in public speaking, regardless of their field, often advanced more quickly. Whether it was politicians, lawyers, business leaders, or community organizers, their ability to captivate and persuade an audience played a crucial role in their success. Public speaking wasn't just an asset but a necessity. I realized that mastering this skill would help me professionally and be a powerful catalyst for my intellectual, social, and personal development.

It became clear to me that public speaking is about far more than just delivering a polished presentation. It is an art form that sharpens your mind, enhances your ability to connect with others, and fuels personal growth. With every speech I delivered—whether a formal presentation or an impromptu talk—I grew more confident, articulate, and aware of the power my words could have on others.

A SKILL FOR EVERY FIELD

Throughout history, oratory skills have been a foundation for many careers. It's easy to see why public speaking is indispensable for professionals in fields such as politics, law, business, nonprofit work, and ministry. What often goes unnoticed is how valuable these skills are across every profession. As our society increasingly values communication and connection, the ability to speak effectively in public becomes even more critical.

I've witnessed how public speaking provides valuable training for the workforce, especially where strong communication skills are in high demand. Sadly, many young people today view public speaking as irrelevant or worse as a task too difficult to master. In schools, the focus on standardized testing has squeezed out opportunities for activities such as public speaking, which fosters well-rounded, confident individuals.

When I reflect on the students who resist the challenge of public speaking, I can't help but think of the missed potential. These young people have the opportunity to strengthen their ability to communicate effectively but many avoid it out of fear or a belief that it isn't important. When I look at the most successful people in any field, I see that their ability to stand up, speak clearly, and persuade an audience has been crucial to their success.

A LEGACY IN THE BLACK EXPERIENCE

For Black Americans, public speaking has held particular significance. The power of oratory has been a pillar of activism and leadership, shaping the course of history. Figures such as Frederick Douglass, Dr. Martin Luther King Jr., Malcolm X, and President Barack Obama have used their voices to challenge oppression and inspire change. Public speaking became one of the most powerful tools in the fight for freedom, justice, and equality.

This tradition of oratory is woven into the fabric of Black American history. Public speaking wasn't just a skill but rather a weapon and form of resistance. It allowed Black leaders to mobilize communities, challenge systemic injustices, and shape the future. The richness of this tradition cemented speaking as one of the most important means of communicating within the Black community. It was a way to challenge the dominant narrative and fight against the inferiority that was imposed by society.

I have always admired how public speaking has been a source of empowerment for Black individuals. With each speech, a new image was sculpted—one of dignity, strength, and leadership. Every speech motivated and instructed, bound together families and communities, and ignited movements that changed the course of history. The art of public speaking helped shape the identity of the Black individual, the community, and eventually the race.

FROM FEAR TO CONFIDENCE

As I embarked on my own journey with public speaking, I realized how transformative it could be on a personal level. At first, I faced the same fears and doubts that many others do. With time, I saw that public speaking was a pathway to overcoming those fears. The more I spoke, the more confident I became. It wasn't just about delivering information but rather finding my voice, owning my story, and commanding attention in a way that was authentic to me.

I learned that confidence was key. No audience appreciates a speaker who lacks conviction in what they are saying. It became clear that the best speakers aren't necessarily the most polished. They are the ones who believe deeply in their message. Confidence is contagious. When you believe in what you're saying, your audience will too. As I grew more confident, I began to see public speaking as an opportunity, not a burden.

Along the way, I also discovered the importance of body language. Public speaking is more than just words. It's about how you carry yourself. Mastering gestures, facial expressions, and physical presence is critical to delivering a message that resonates. I realized that to truly connect with an audience, my body had to communicate just as clearly as my voice.

PUBLIC SPEAKING: A UNIVERSAL TOOL

Public speaking transcends race, culture, and profession. Its power has shaped civilizations, influenced revolutions, and propelled great leaders to the forefront of history. From the Black preachers of the early abolitionist movement to the orators of the

Civil Rights Era, public speaking has been a tool for inspiring, mobilizing, and leading.

In my experience, I've seen how public speaking can lead to immense personal growth. Whether it's speaking up at work, presenting at a conference, or engaging in a community forum, these opportunities sharpen critical thinking, enhance leadership abilities, and foster greater self-awareness. Through speaking, I have grown more confident in my ability to lead, more aware of my strengths, and more capable of handling diverse situations.

A CALL TO ACTION

Public speaking is not a skill reserved for a select few but rather a tool that everyone should develop. In a world where communication is more important than ever, the ability to express yourself clearly and powerfully is invaluable. It opens doors, builds relationships, and creates opportunities for growth. I encourage everyone, especially young people, to embrace public speaking as a way to unlock their potential.

As I continue to develop my skills as a speaker, I am reminded of the rich history and legacy that comes with public oratory. It is a tool that has shaped the course of history and continues to impact individuals every day. For those willing to overcome their fear and embrace this skill, the professional and personal rewards are endless.

Public speaking is a path to leadership, empowerment, and self-discovery. Through practice and perseverance, I've learned that the ability to speak confidently in front of others is one of the most valuable skills we can develop. As I reflect on my own journey, I can see how far I've come and how much further there is to go.

10

Gratitude–
The Heart of a Fulfilling Life

*Gratitude is not just an emotion
but a way of seeing the world.*
Dr. Thurman E. Webb, Jr.

I USED TO THINK THAT SUCCESS CAME FROM HARD WORK alone and that if I put in enough effort, I could shape my life into something meaningful. As I've grown and reflected on my journey, I've come to realize that the true key to a wonderful life isn't just determination or drive but rather gratitude. Gratitude is what ties it all together. It's the secret ingredient that transforms the ordinary into the extraordinary, deepens relationships, and turns challenges into opportunities for growth.

Gratitude is more than just a simple thank-you. It's a way of seeing the world. It's about recognizing the value of what we receive, even in the small moments. I remember the first time I truly grasped the power of gratitude. It wasn't in some grand gesture or life-changing event but in the quiet, everyday exchanges with the people around me. A friend's unexpected help, a colleague's thoughtful advice, or even a kind word from a stranger made me feel a sense of connection, of being seen and valued. In return, I wanted to give back, to express my appreciation and strengthen those bonds.

In many ways, gratitude is the glue that holds our relationships together. It's not just about being thankful for gifts or favors but rather acknowledging the effort, care, and generosity of others. When we practice gratitude, we're nurturing our relationships and reinforcing the positive energy that keeps them strong. It's a cycle that lifts both the giver and the receiver.

I've learned that gratitude isn't a one-way street. When we express it, we not only uplift others but also enhance our own sense of well-being. It's a reminder we are not alone and that our lives are deeply intertwined with those around us. As the saying goes, "No man is an island." Our connections with others are what shape our experiences. When we pause to appreciate those connections, life becomes richer, fuller, and more meaningful.

GRATITUDE IN A CULTURE OF INDEPENDENCE

One of the challenges I've faced is that we live in a culture that often values independence over interdependence. From an early age, we're taught to be self-reliant, pull ourselves up by our bootstraps, and succeed on our own. Where does that leave gratitude? If we believe we have to do everything ourselves, it's easy to overlook the help we receive from others. We miss out on the chance to acknowledge the support that has played a role in our success.

I too once fell into this mindset. I prided myself on being independent, rarely asking for help. As I've grown, I've realized that self-reliance is not the same as thriving. Gratitude taught me that it's okay, even necessary, to acknowledge the contributions of others. None of us gets to where we are entirely on our own. Every step forward, every achievement, is shaped by the people who walk with us, support us, and help us grow.

This realization was humbling. It shifted my perspective from one of striving alone to one of appreciating the connections and relationships that have made my journey possible. Gratitude became a way to honor those who have helped me and recognize that success is never a solo act but rather a collective effort. With that recognition came a sense of peace and fulfillment I hadn't expected.

THE POWER OF REFLECTION AND CONNECTION

As I began to practice gratitude more intentionally, I noticed how it impacted my life in profound ways. I started with small steps, taking a few moments each day to reflect on the things I was thankful for. Sometimes it was something as simple as a peaceful morning or a good conversation with a friend. Other times, it was the realization of how much I had grown because of the challenges I had faced.

What surprised me most was how this practice shifted my outlook on life. Instead of focusing on what I didn't have or what wasn't going right, I became more aware of the abundance around me. Even in difficult times, I could find something to be grateful for, be it a lesson learned, a new perspective gained, or the strength I found in myself. Gratitude became my anchor, grounding me when life felt uncertain and helping me stay connected to what truly mattered.

I've learned that gratitude is a social emotion. It binds us to others, reinforcing the connections that make life meaningful. It's not just about the act of saying thank you. It's instead about recognizing the impact that people have on our lives. When we do that, something amazing happens. Our relationships deepen, our sense of community strengthens, and we become more attuned to the beauty in the world around us.

A PRACTICE FOR A FULFILLING LIFE

Over time, I realized that gratitude is not something that just happens but instead must be cultivated. It requires mindfulness and intentionality. I started looking for the good in my day, even when it wasn't obvious. This wasn't always easy. Like everyone, I had my share of bad days, disappointments, and frustrations. But I found that by acknowledging those difficulties and then reflecting on the things I still had to be grateful for, my perspective shifted.

I learned to balance the reality of life's challenges with a mindset of appreciation. In fact, acknowledging the hard times made my gratitude even more powerful. It helped me realize just how much I had to be thankful for, even in the midst of struggles. This mindset helped me stay grounded, stop focusing on what I lacked and start appreciating what I had.

It's easy to take things for granted and to move so quickly through life that we forget to pause and reflect on the blessings we've received. When we make the choice to practice gratitude, we open the door to a life of greater joy, peace, and fulfillment. It's not about ignoring the challenges but about choosing to see the good that exists alongside them.

DR. THURMAN E. WEBB, JR.

GRATITUDE AT WORK AND BEYOND

Gratitude isn't just a personal practice. It extends into every area of life, including the workplace. I've found that expressing gratitude in professional settings toward colleagues, clients, or mentors creates a positive environment where people feel valued. In a highly competitive world, showing appreciation for others' contributions can make all the difference. It fosters a sense of belonging, encourages collaboration, and ultimately leads to greater success.

In my career, I've seen how gratitude enhances productivity and strengthens relationships. People who feel appreciated are more likely to be engaged, motivated, and committed to their work. Gratitude, in this sense, is not just a nice gesture but rather a powerful tool for building a positive and supportive workplace culture.

GRATITUDE AS THE KEY TO A WONDERFUL LIFE

Looking back, I realize that gratitude has been the key ingredient in creating a wonderful life. It's what has helped me navigate challenges, deepen my relationships, and find joy in the everyday moments. Gratitude is not just a feeling but a way of being. It reminds us that we are not alone, that we are supported by the kindness and generosity of others, and that life is filled with moments of grace.

By practicing gratitude, I have found greater meaning and fulfillment in my life. It has shaped the way I see the world and the way I engage with the people around me. In the end, gratitude is not just something we express, it's something we live. When we live with gratitude, we unlock the true richness of life.

Debriefing

Part V of *Be Still, Say Less* focuses on mastering stillness within a rapidly changing world. It emphasizes the importance of self-leadership, adaptability, and personal growth as foundational elements for navigating chaos and creating a lasting legacy. This section moves beyond personal empowerment to exploring how individuals can leverage their inner-strength to thrive in complex environments and influence future generations.

KEY THEMES

- **Cultivating Self-Leadership in a Changing World:** This pillar stresses that true leadership begins with leading oneself. It emphasizes self-awareness, adaptability, and personal responsibility as essential for navigating the dynamic landscape of life. It highlights that leadership is not about titles but about taking ownership of one's actions and inspiring others through personal example, especially within marginalized communities.

- **The Art of Letting Go: Embracing Self-Awareness, Delegation, and Empowered Leadership:** This section explores delegation as more than just task assignment. It's a tool for self-awareness, recognizing strengths and limitations, and trusting others. Effective delegation empowers both the delegator and the delegate, fostering growth and collaboration. It's about managing energy and resources efficiently to focus on core strengths and long-term goals.
- **Transforming Conflict: Leading Through Creative Abrasion:** This pillar views conflict as an opportunity for deeper understanding and growth. It emphasizes empathy, active listening, and collaboration as crucial for resolving conflict constructively. The goal is to find "win-win" solutions that strengthen relationships and foster a sense of shared purpose, turning conflict into a catalyst for positive change.
- **Harnessing Emotional Intelligence for Personal Growth and Fulfillment:** This section highlights the importance of emotional intelligence in navigating life's challenges. It emphasizes self-awareness, self-regulation, motivation, empathy, and social skills as key components of emotional intelligence. Developing it leads to healthier relationships, better decision-making, and a more balanced approach to personal and professional growth.
- **Growing Through Change: The Power of Adaptability:** This pillar stresses the necessity of adaptability in an ever-evolving world. It focuses on embracing change, continuous learning, and emotional resilience. Adaptability is seen as a key to unlocking growth, turning challenges into opportunities, and fostering innovation.

- **Unlocking Potential with a Growth Mindset:** This section explores the concept of a growth mindset, which believes that abilities can be developed through effort and perseverance. It encourages embracing challenges, learning from mistakes, and committing to lifelong learning. A growth mindset fosters resilience, drives innovation, and leads to greater personal and professional success.
- **The Role of Risk-Taking in Personal and Professional Growth:** This pillar examines risk-taking as an essential element of growth and empowerment. It emphasizes calculated risks, embracing uncertainty, and pushing beyond comfort zones. It also touches on the historical context of risk-taking within marginalized communities, particularly Black America, and its connection to entrepreneurship and challenging systemic injustice.

Part V is about mastering stillness amidst chaos by developing internal strength, adaptability, and a forward-thinking mindset. It encourages readers to do the following.

- **Lead themselves effectively** by understanding their values and purpose.
- **Delegate with intention** to empower others and focus on core strengths.
- **Transform conflict constructively** by fostering empathy and collaboration.
- **Harness emotional intelligence** for personal growth and healthier relationships.

- **Embrace change and adaptability** as opportunities for innovation and progress.
- **Cultivate a growth mindset** to unlock their full potential and learn from challenges.
- **Take calculated risks** to pursue opportunities and create a lasting impact.

In summary, Part V is a guide to navigating a complex world with grace and purpose. It emphasizes that true mastery lies in inner-development, allowing individuals to lead themselves and others effectively, adapt to change, and leave a positive legacy.

AFFIRMATION

I cultivate self-leadership, embrace change with adaptability, and unlock my potential through a growth mindset. I transform conflict into understanding, harness my emotional intelligence, and take calculated risks to create a lasting and impactful legacy.

SELF- REFLECTION

Part V of *Be Still, Say Less* focuses on navigating a changing world with self-leadership, adaptability, and a growth mindset. It's about moving from personal empowerment to leveraging inner-strength for broader impact. Take time to reflect on the following questions to deepen your understanding and application of these themes.

1. **Cultivating Self-Leadership in a Changing World:**
   - How do I currently lead myself? Am I proactive or reactive in my approach to life?

- Do I take ownership of my actions and decisions? Where might I be avoiding responsibility?
- How do I adapt to changes in my personal and professional life? Am I resistant or open to new circumstances?
- Do I inspire others through my actions and example? How can I enhance my influence in positive ways?
- In what areas of my life do I feel most in control? Where do I feel I lack leadership over myself?
- What steps can I take to strengthen my self-leadership skills?

2. The Art of Letting Go: Embracing Self-Awareness, Delegation, and Empowered Leadership:
- Am I aware of my strengths and limitations? Where am I trying to do everything myself?
- Do I effectively delegate tasks and responsibilities? What holds me back from delegating?
- Do I trust others to handle tasks or do I feel I must always be in control?
- How can I better manage my time and energy by delegating?
- Am I empowering others when I delegate or just assigning tasks?
- What tasks could I delegate this week to free up my time and energy?

3. Transforming Conflict: Leading Through Creative Abrasion:
- How do I typically respond to conflict? Do I avoid it, confront it aggressively, or seek collaboration?

- Am I able to understand others' perspectives during conflict? Do I practice active listening?
- How can I transform conflict into opportunities for growth and understanding?
- Can I recall a recent conflict? What could I have done differently to achieve a "win-win" outcome?
- Am I willing to find common ground and seek solutions that benefit everyone involved?
- What steps can I take to improve my conflict resolution skills?

4. Harnessing Emotional Intelligence for Personal Growth and Fulfillment:
- How aware am I of my own emotions? Can I identify my emotional triggers?
- Am I able to regulate my emotions in challenging situations? How do I manage stress and anxiety?
- Am I motivated by intrinsic factors (purpose, fulfillment) or extrinsic factors (rewards, recognition)?
- Do I practice empathy in my interactions with others? Do I understand and share their feelings?
- How would I rate my social skills? How can I improve my ability to manage relationships and navigate social situations?
- What steps can I take to develop my emotional intelligence further?

5. Growing Through Change: The Power of Adaptability:
- How do I typically respond to change? Am I resistant or open to new situations?

- Do I embrace continuous learning and seek out new information and experiences?
- Am I able to let go of old habits and mindsets that no longer serve me?
- How do I perceive uncertainty? Do I fear it or see it as an opportunity for growth?
- In what areas of my life do I need to be more adaptable?
- What steps can I take to cultivate greater adaptability in my daily life?

6. Unlocking Potential with a Growth Mindset:

- Do I believe that my abilities and intelligence are fixed or can be developed?
- How do I respond to challenges and setbacks? Do I see them as opportunities or failures?
- Am I committed to lifelong learning? Do I actively seek out new knowledge and skills?
- Do I view mistakes as learning opportunities or reasons to give up?
- How can I shift from a fixed mindset to a growth mindset in different areas of my life?
- What steps can I take to foster a growth mindset in my work, relationships, and personal development?

7. The Role of Risk-Taking in Personal and Professional Growth:

- How do I perceive risk? Am I risk-averse or willing to take calculated risks?
- Do I push beyond my comfort zone and embrace uncertainty?

- Am I aware of the historical context of risk-taking, especially within marginalized communities?
- How can I balance caution with courage when making decisions?
- What risks have I taken in the past that have led to personal or professional growth?
- What risks am I currently considering, and what is holding me back?

Overall Reflection:
- How am I currently mastering stillness in my life? Where do I need improvement?
- What key insights have I gained from reflecting on Part V?
- What specific action steps will I take to implement these insights and cultivate self-leadership, adaptability, and a growth mindset?
- How will I hold myself accountable for these changes?
- What kind of legacy do I want to leave, and how can mastering stillness contribute to that legacy?

This self-reflection will help you apply the principles of Part V to your own life, fostering personal growth, effective leadership, and resilience in an ever-changing world. Remember to be honest, compassionate, and open to new possibilities during this process.

Conclusion

BE STILL, SAY LESS INVITES US ON A TRANSFORMATIVE odyssey, a journey that begins with the essential, often challenging, act of profound self-discovery and ultimately culminates in crafting a lasting legacy that resonates far beyond our individual existence. We embarked on this path by first diving deep into the realm of self-awareness, recognizing it as the bedrock upon which all genuine personal growth is built. Here, we learned the importance of acknowledging our innermost truths, confronting the shadows of past traumas, and consciously shifting our perceptions to cultivate perspectives that empower and uplift. This initial exploration was not merely introspective but foundational, laying the critical groundwork for understanding the dynamic interplay of time, intention, and impact, reminding us that each moment is an invaluable, finite resource to be wielded with wisdom and purpose.

Building upon this foundation of self-knowledge, we transitioned to the art of cultivating stillness in our interactions with the world. We delved into the nuances of forging meaningful connections, learning to trust the intuitive compass within, and diligently resolving past unfinished business to foster a life characterized by peace, authenticity, and genuine engagement. This phase emphasized the critical role of curating our relationships, maintaining a sanctuary of inner tranquility, and honoring the profound wisdom of our instincts. We acknowledged that our interactions with others are not separate from our individual journey but rather integral to it, shaping and being shaped by our evolving selves.

During our journey we entered quiet transformation, a realm where we were challenged to redefine success on our own terms, liberating ourselves from societal constructs and aligning our actions with the unwavering compass of our core values. We grasped that true fulfillment transcends external accolades, arising instead from living authentically, prioritizing our holistic well-being, and making deliberate, conscious choices that echo our deepest selves. This section was a potent call to action, urging us to seize the reins of our lives, to own our narratives, and to sculpt our futures with unwavering intention and purpose.

At one point, we two-stepped into the space of empowered presence, understanding that our inner-work is not meant to remain internal but must be embodied and vibrantly expressed in our interactions with the world. We diligently cultivated resilience, practiced gratitude as a way of life, strategically leveraged mentorship, and forged authentic connections, recognizing that our individual strength and impact are exponentially amplified when we engage with others from a place of genuine authenticity and profound interconnectedness. This phase was about transmuting personal transformation into a tangible force, living from a place of unwavering strength, clarity, and purpose.

Finally, as we headed toward the finish line, the final section challenged us to contemplate our legacy of presence, urging us to transcend the confines of our individual lives and envision the ripple effect of our actions on future generations. We explored the nuances of self-leadership, the necessity of adaptability in a chaotic world, the power of a growth mindset, and the wisdom of taking calculated risks to forge a lasting and impactful legacy. We understood that mastering stillness in a world of constant flux meant embracing change as an ally, transforming conflict into an opportunity for growth, and harnessing emotional intelligence to lead ourselves and others with integrity, compassion, and unwavering purpose. This final section was a powerful call to extend our influence beyond our immediate circles, to leave an indelible positive mark on the world, and to empower those who follow in our footsteps.

Throughout our amazing race, the enduring threads of self-reflection, unwavering accountability, and a commitment to continuous learning have served as our guiding stars. We have come to realize that true success is not a fixed destination but a dynamic, ever-evolving process of growth, fueled by intentional choices and a profound, ever-deepening understanding of ourselves. We have discovered that by embracing stillness and speaking less, we can more clearly hear the whispers of our inner-wisdom, navigate the complexities of life with grace and equanimity, and create a life that not only resonates with personal fulfillment but also leaves a positive and enduring impact on the world around us.

Be Still, Say Less is more than just a collection of words. It is a comprehensive roadmap, a deeply personal guide to living an authentic, purposeful, and impactful life. It is an invitation to slow down in a world that moves too fast, to listen deeply to the quiet voice within, and to act with unwavering intention, trusting that the answers we seek are often nestled within the stillness of our own hearts. As you carry these lessons forward, remember that you possess the innate power to shape your own destiny, to forge meaningful and lasting connections, and to leave a legacy that inspires others to embark on their own journeys of self-discovery and transformation. Now, go forth and live the life you were meant to live with intention, purpose, and unwavering presence.

Afterword

As we conclude this journey through the pillars of success, I leave you with one final yet fundamental challenge: Embrace awareness and accountability as the keys to unlocking your fullest potential.

Awareness is more than knowledge. It is a call to action. To see yourself clearly–to recognize your habits, your strengths, and your blind spots–is to take ownership of your growth. It is not always comfortable. In fact, true awareness often brings discomfort because it demands accountability. It strips away excuses, dissolves self-imposed limitations, and forces us to confront the reality that we are in control of far more than we once believed.

That is where the real transformation begins. When you move beyond discomfort and into action, you awaken a power within yourself that no external force can shake. This is the internal locus of control, the unshakable belief that you are not at the mercy of circumstances but rather the architect of your own reality. With this mindset, obstacles become challenges to overcome rather than roadblocks that define you. Failures become lessons, not defeats. Success becomes not a destination but a continuous process of growth driven by the choices you make every single day.

As you step away from these pages and back into the world, I encourage you to own your influence. No matter where you stand today, no matter what challenges lie ahead, remember that because you are who you are, you have the power to shape everything around you. Let that truth guide your actions, fuel your resilience, and propel you toward the success that is already within your reach.

Now, go do the work.

About the Author

Dr. Thurman E. Webb, Jr., is the CEO of Centered Person Consulting, a firm dedicated to helping individuals and organizations exceed their existing capabilities through personalized critical lens development. Centered Person Consulting is committed to equipping clients with the necessary tools to diversify thinking and enhance both individual and collective perspectives, challenging them to overcome self-imposed limitations. The firm specializes in increasing self-reflective awareness, enhancing leadership and communication, and building cultural competency, thereby fostering culturally responsive leadership and improving engagement and performance across various sectors.

Dr. Webb is an esteemed executive coach and facilitator at the Energy Project, leveraging his skills as a licensed therapist and industrial and organizational psychologist. His strategic expertise has been sought after by notable organizations including Lincoln Financial Group; Park and Battery Global Advertising; and financial advisors at Northwestern Mutual, where he has significantly enhanced leadership awareness and team collaboration.

In his executive coaching and mental performance consulting

practice, Thurman has notably advanced the mental performance and awareness of Grammy Award-winning artists and numerous professional athletes, tailoring coaching experiences to enhance their self-efficacy by boosting efficiency, performance, and productivity.

Having also served as a tenured professor of psychology at Tennessee State University, Dr. Webb demonstrates a profound commitment to mental wellness and the advancement of psychological understanding and application. His work, both in academia and in the field, establishes him as a pivotal figure in the realms of psychology and executive coaching.

Call to Action

Act on what you know and identify purpose.

Reflection and Mindfulness:
- Set aside time each day for self-reflection.
- Practice mindfulness meditation to stay present in the moment.

Journaling:
- Maintain a daily journal to record thoughts, feelings, and experiences.
- Regularly review and analyze journal entries for patterns and insights.

Feedback Seeking:
- Solicit feedback from friends, family, and colleagues.
- Be open to constructive criticism and use it as an opportunity for growth.

Personality Assessments:
- Take reputable personality assessments (e.g., Myers-Briggs, DISC, Big Five, enneagram).
- Reflect on the results and identify areas for personal development.

Values Clarification:
- Define your core values and principles.
- Align your actions and decisions with these values.

Goal Setting:
- Set clear and realistic short-term and long-term goals.
- Regularly assess progress and adjust goals as needed.

Emotional Intelligence Development:
- Identify and label your emotions accurately.
- Practice empathy and understand the emotions of others.

Seek Different Perspectives:
- Engage in conversations with people from diverse backgrounds.
- Consider different viewpoints to broaden your understanding.

Continuous Learning:
- Stay curious and actively seek new knowledge.
- Embrace challenges as opportunities for growth.

Mind-Body Connection:
- Pay attention to physical sensations and how they relate to emotions.

- Incorporate activities such as exercise and proper nutrition for overall well-being.

Time Management:
- Assess how you spend your time and prioritize tasks.
- Ensure alignment between your activities and personal values.

Constructive Self-Talk:
- Monitor your internal dialogue and challenge negative thoughts.
- Cultivate a positive and empowering mindset.

Networking:
- Build a diverse network of relationships.
- Gain insights from others and share your experiences.

Celebrate Successes and Learn from Failures:
- Acknowledge achievements and milestones.
- Learn from setbacks and use them as opportunities for improvement.

Regular Check-Ins:
- Schedule periodic self-assessments to track personal growth.
- Adjust strategies based on evolving self-awareness.

www.ingramcontent.com/pod-product-compliance
Lightning Source LLC
Chambersburg PA
CBHW072115050526
44107CB00098BA/195